THE VEGAN ZOMBIE
COOK & SURVIVE!

CHRIS COONEY
AND **JON TEDD**

ILLUSTRATED BY
ROB KRAMER

The Vegan Zombie
Cook & Survive!
© 2013 Chris Cooney & Jon Tedd

1st printing November 2013

Photography
Chris Cooney

Art & Illustration
Rob Kramer

Graphic Design & Layout
Justin P. Moore
www.lotusartichoke.com

Printing & Binding
freiburger graphische betriebe
Printed in Germany

ISBN 978-3-95575-013-8
© for this edition Ventil Verlag UG (haftungsbeschränkt) & Co. KG
Edition Kochen ohne Knochen

Ventil Verlag
Boppstr. 25
55118 Mainz
Germany
www.ventil-verlag.de

www.theveganzombie.com
facebook.com/ZombieGate
youtube.com/ZombieGate

COOK & SURVIVE!

Zombies walk among us every day. They feast on whatever they can get their hands on. Some eat brains. Some eat grains.

You must be wondering: How can you stay safe and not become like them?

How can I get my hands on quick and easy, super tasty recipes to guarantee survival in even the worst zombie apocalypse?

Well, look no further than this cookbook!

After years of indulging myself into the realm of the horror genre and making short movies and videos with friends and family, I decided to incorporate that, along with my vegan lifestyle. The idea of a zombie outbreak, in which consuming animal products, meat and dairy, as the cause of infection, immediately came to mind. Our now popular YouTube show, The Vegan Zombie, which is nothing short of a comical cooking show set in a zombie apocalypse, was born. Since its creation, I have had countless requests to put together a cookbook featuring our online recipes. I took it into consideration and started putting together the concept for this cookbook. With the overwhelming success of our crowdfunding venture, and with the help of our talented artist, Rob, this book has become a reality! Ultimately, everything was made possible by you, the fans!

Along with my good friend Jon, we put together this cooking survival guide to help you and your loved ones create delicious zombie-free dishes. There is something in here for everyone: comfort foods, desserts, healthy dishes, brunch ideas and more. We've even got a fully-illustrated story in here for you!

If you follow our directions and make the mouth-watering meals from this survival cookbook, you'll always stay one step ahead of the mindless undead.

STAY SAFE!

Chris Cooney

COMMUNICATION SYSTEMS AS WE KNEW HAD FAILED.

I HAD TO LEAVE MY APARTMENT TO FIND FOOD, SURVIVORS, AND, MOST OF ALL, ANSWERS.

A... KITCHEN!

DON'T CUT MY FINGERS OFF—

DON'T BURN MY FACE OFF...

MMM...

UNGHHHH

OF COURSE— THINGS WERE TOO QUIET.

MY GUN! • • •

GHOMP

NOT SO SANITARY.

BUT-- WE'LL JUST FIND A NEW SAFEHOUSE!

HE SAVED MY LIFE, AND I NAMED THAT PUP INDY.

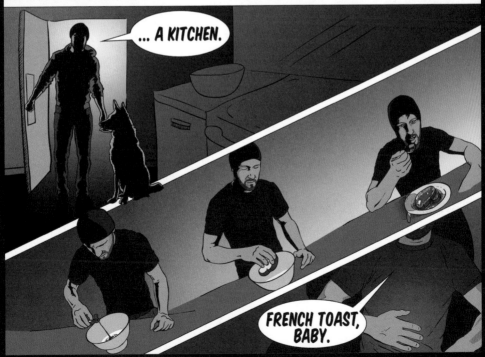

WE RAN...

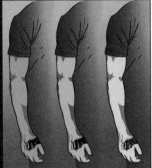

I HAVE NEVER FELT A MORE EXCRUCIATING PAIN. WHEN I AWOKE HOURS LATER INDY HAD STAYED...

I DON'T WANT TO EAT YOUR FACE... THAT'S GOOD!

1. GATHER
2. MEASURE
3. MIX
4. KNEAD
5. FORM
6. BAKE

HEY GUYS, DO YOU SMELL THAT?
THERE'S NO WAY A ZOMBIE IS BAKING!
COULD IT BE... ANOTHER...
SURVIVOR?!
SURVIVORS?!
INDY!
ZOMBIE CREW

TO BE CONTINUED...

BREAKFAST

APPLE CIDER PANCAKES

MAKES 4 TO 6 PANCAKES • TIME 15 MIN

APPLE TOPPING

4 granny smith apples thinly sliced
2 Tbs refined coconut oil
1/4 cup (60 g) sugar
1 1/2 tsp cinnamon
1/4 tsp sea salt

1. Heat coconut oil in saucepan on medium heat.

2. Add sliced apples, sugar, cinnamon and sea salt to pan.
   Cook stirring and turning often until apples are soft, about 10–15 min.

PANCAKE BATTER

1 1/4 cups (190 g) flour
2 tsp baking powder
1 1/2 tsp cinnamon
1/4 tsp nutmeg
1 tsp sea salt
1 1/3 cups (320 ml) apple cider (non-alcoholic)
1 tsp vanilla
1 tsp coconut nectar or **agave nectar**
1 Tbs canola oil

1. In medium size mixing bowl, add flour, baking powder, cinnamon, nutmeg and
   sea salt. Whisk together.

2. In separate bowl, add apple cider, vanilla, coconut nectar and canola oil.
   Whisk liquid ingredients together.

3. Pour the wet into the dry and lightly mix. Don't over mix batter.

4. Heat nonstick skillet on medium heat. Very lightly coat skillet with oil or vegan
   butter.

5. Pour batter on skillet to form pancakes. Flip after 1–2 min or until browned,
   depending on the heat of your stove.

ZOMBIE-FREE FRENCH TOAST

SERVES 4 • TIME 15 MIN

1 loaf stale bread thick slices
1 cup (240 ml) soy milk
1/4 cup (40 g) flour
1/4 cup (40 g) powdered sugar
1 Tbs corn starch
2 Tbs maple syrup or **agave nectar**
1 tsp vanilla extract
1 tsp cinnamon
1/8 tsp sea salt
1 Tbs coconut oil
1–2 bananas thinly sliced OPTIONAL

1. In mixing bowl, add soymilk, flour, powdered sugar, corn starch, agave nectar, vanilla extract, cinnamon and sea salt. Whisk everything together.

2. Heat nonstick pan on medium heat. Lightly coat with coconut oil.

3. Dip slices of bread in the batter and place in heated pan. Cook each side until golden brown, about 2 min. Transfer to plate.

4. Add banana slices, and dust with powdered sugar. Top with maple syrup or agave nectar.

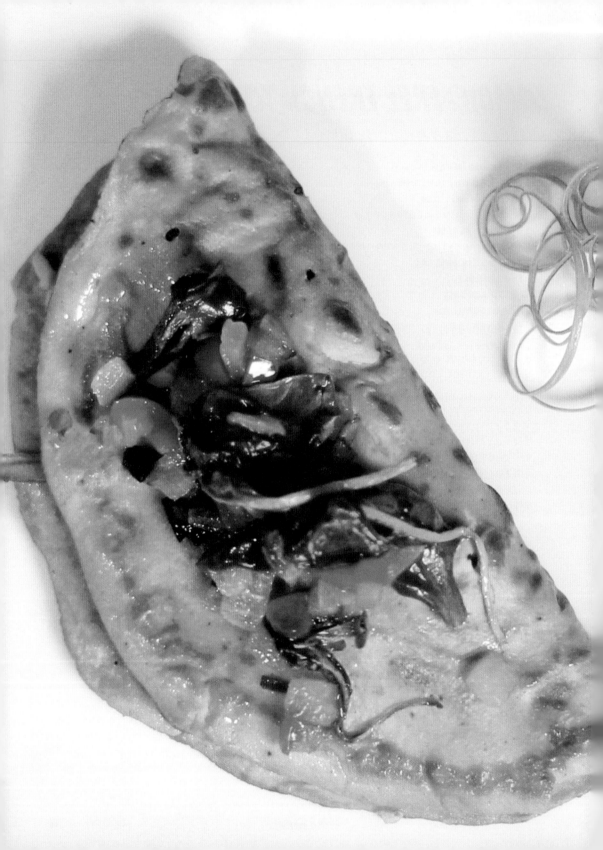

THE VEGAN ZOMBLETTE

MAKES 4 OR 5 OMELETS • TIME 20 MIN

2 Tbs olive oil
8 oz (225 g) fresh firm tofu
1 Tbs nutritional yeast flakes
1 tsp corn starch
2 Tbs chickpea flour
1/2 tsp curry powder
1/8 tsp sea salt
1/8 tsp black pepper
1/8 tsp paprika
1/8 tsp dried sage
1 tsp onion powder
1 tsp Dijon mustard
1 tsp The Wizard's Organic Worcestershire Sauce
3–5 Tbs veggie broth (page 159)
1/2 tsp hot sauce OPTIONAL
1 cup (30 g) fresh spinach chopped
1/2 Tbs olive oil
1/4 cup (30 g) green pepper chopped
1/4 cup (30 g) red pepper chopped
1/4 cup (30 g) yellow pepper chopped
1–2 shallots chopped
1/2 cup (50 g) vegan cheese shreds

1. In a high-powered blender (e.g. Blendtec) add tofu, nutritional yeast, corn starch, chickpea flour, curry powder, salt, pepper, paprika, sage, onion powder, mustard, Worcestershire sauce, veggie broth and hot sauce. Blend on high until smooth, about 45 sec. If too thick, add more veggie broth until you get a thick pancake batter consistency. How well you drained your tofu will affect this.

2. Pour batter in mixing bowl. Stir in choppped spinach.

3. Lightly coat nonstick pan with olive oil. Put it on low heat and pour batter on pan. Spread it out so it's no larger than 6 in (15 cm) in diameter. Cover and cook 5–6 min.

4. Heat olive oil on medium low heat in seperate frying pan. Add peppers and shallot; sauté until lightly browned, 2–3 min.

5. Carefully flip omelet with spatula. Reduce to low heat. Cover and cook another 5 min. Add vegan shreds and sautéed veggies to omelet. Cover again and cook another 2–3 min. Fold omelet over keeping the vegan cheese and veggies in the middle. Garnish with more sautéed veggies and freshly chopped spinach.

TOFU SCRAMBLE

SERVES 2 TO 3 • TIME 15 MIN

2 Tbs olive oil
1–2 small onions chopped
16 oz (450 g) extra firm tofu
1 tsp garlic powder
1 tsp dried sage
1/2 tsp turmeric
1 tsp ground cumin
1 tsp paprika
1/4 cup (20 g) nutritional yeast flakes
1 Tbs mustard OPTIONAL
1 tsp The Wizard's Organic Worcestershire Sauce
1 Roma tomato chopped
1 cup (30 g) fresh spinach chopped

1. Heat oil in frying pan on a medium heat. Add onions, sauté 5 min. Roughly break up tofu into small and medium chunks and add to frying pan. Add garlic powder, sage, turmeric, cumin, paprika, nutritional yeast, Worcestershire sauce and mustard. Stir until tofu is a nice yellowish color. Cook 3–4 min.

2. Stir in the chopped tomato and spinach, cover and cook 2–3 min, mixing ocassionally to prevent it from sticking and burning. Remove from heat.

3. Serve with hot sauce if desired.

BREAKFAST BURRITO

MAKES 4 BURRITOS • TIME 25 MIN

2 Tbs olive oil
2 medium / 1 cup (140 g) potatoes chopped
1/2 tsp sea salt
1/2 tsp black pepper
1/2 tsp dried thyme
1/2 tsp dried basil
3 Tbs vegan bacon bits
OR **coconut bacon** (page 165) OPTIONAL
1/2 medium onion chopped
16 oz (450 g) extra firm tofu
1 tsp turmeric
1 tsp garlic powder
1/2 tsp paprika
1/4 cup (20 g) nutritional yeast flakes
1 tsp The Wizard's Organic Worcestershire Sauce OPTIONAL
1/4 cup tomato chopped
1/4 cup (25 g) vegan cheese shreds
1 cup (30 g) fresh spinach chopped
1 Tbs hot sauce OPTIONAL
4 tortilla shells

1. Heat oil in frying pan on medium heat. Add potatoes, thyme, basil, salt and pepper. Cook, stirring constantly, 5 min. Add onions, vegan bacon. Cook another 2–3 min.

2. Crumble tofu into medium small pieces and add to frying pan. Stir well. Add turmeric, garlic powder, paprika, nutritional yeast and Worcestershire sauce and stir together. Cook 2 to 3 min. Stir in tomato, spinach and vegan cheese. Cover and remove from heat.

3. Warm tortilla shells and scoop tofu mixture onto shell. Add hot sauce and roll up to form your breakfast burrito.

EGG TRICK MUFFIN created by Strong Hearts Cafe

MAKES 4 • TIME 20 MIN

14 oz (400 g) extra firm tofu
1/2 cup (40 g) nutritional yeast flakes
2 tsp turmeric
1/2 tsp garlic powder
1/2 tsp onion powder
1/2 tsp sea salt
2–3 Tbs canola oil
14 oz (400 g) vegan sausage
or **4–8 vegan ham slices**
1 cup / 4 oz (100 g) vegan cheese shreds
4 English muffins

1. With 3 in (8 cm) circular cookie cutter, cut through tofu, making a cylinder shape. Slice horizontally into thirds for 3 hockey puck shaped pieces of tofu. (Remaining tofu can be used for tofu scramble or other recipes.)

2. In mixing bowl, combine nutritional yeast, turmeric, garlic powder, onion powder and salt.

3. Coat tofu discs (which should still be wet) thoroughly with seasoning mix.

4. Heat canola oil in frying pan on medium heat.

5. Form 3 patties with sausage. Place sausage and seasoned tofu in the heated oil and cook 1–2 min until golden brown. Flip over and add vegan cheese to tofu and sausage. Cover and cook another 1–2 min.

6. Toast English muffins.

7. Place tofu on bottom half of English muffin. Place sausage on tofu and top with other muffin half.

Note: Leftover seasoning mixture can be stored for future use.

TEMPEH BACON

MAKES 16 SLICES • TIME 25 MIN

8 oz (225 g) tempeh
3 cups (720 ml) veggie broth (page 159)
1 Tbs liquid smoke
2 Tbs molasses
3 Tbs soy sauce or **liquid aminos**
3 bay leaves
1/2 tsp dried sage
1 tsp chili powder
1 tsp onion powder
3 cloves garlic crushed or finely chopped

1. Slice tempeh into thin strips.

2. Add veggie broth, liquid smoke, molasses, soy sauce, bay leaves, sage, chili powder, onion powder, garlic and tempeh to medium size saucepan. Cover and simmer for 20 min, turning and mixing ocassionally.

   Note: Remaining tempeh may be stored in container with marinade in the fridge.

SALADS & SOUPS

CREAMY KALE SALAD

SERVES 2 TO 4 • TIME 10 MIN

4–5 large stalks of kale
1 red pepper chopped
1 carrot grated
1/4 cup (20 g) nutritional yeast flakes
1/4 cup (40 g) raw slivered almonds
1/2 avocado chopped

DRESSING:
1/2 cup (100 g) sesame tahini
1/2 cup (100 g) raw agave nectar
3–4 Tbs lemon juice
1/2 tsp sea salt OPTIONAL
1 green onion (scallion) Finely chopped
1 Tbs fresh dill Finely chopped

1. Break kale away from stems and place in large salad bowl.

2. Mix in red pepper, carrot and nutritional yeast.

3. In a separate bowl (or blender), mix (or blend) sesame tahini, raw agave nectar, lemon juice, sea salt, green onion, and dill.

4. Pour dressing over salad and gently massage the kale with the dressing 2–3 min.

5. Add avocado and top with almonds.

FRESH PEAR SALAD

SERVES 2 TO 4 • TIME 10 MIN

4–6 cups / 5 oz (140 g) mixed greens
1/2 cup (15 g) radicchio shredded
1 pear thinly sliced
1/2 avocado chopped
1/4 cup (30 g) pine nuts
1/4 cup (30 g) dried cranberries
2 Tbs hemp seeds OPTIONAL

DRESSING:

3 Tbs red onion chopped
2 Tbs lemon juice
2 fresh basil leaves chopped
1 Tbs fresh parsley chopped
1/2 cup (15 g) fresh spinach chopped
1/2 cup (120 ml) extra virgin olive oil
1 Tbs apple cider vinegar
1 Tbs agave nectar
1/2 tsp sea salt
1/2 tsp black pepper

1. Combine the mixed greens, radicchio, cranberries and pine nuts in large salad bowl.

2. Mix red onion, lemon juice, basil, parsley, spinach, olive oil, apple cider vinegar, agave, sea salt and pepper in another bowl. Alternately, blend until smooth in high-powered blender (e.g. Blendtec) about 30 seconds on high.

3. Pour dressing into salad bowl and toss to distribute evenly.

4. Portion salad into 2 large bowls or 4 smaller bowls.

5. Decorate with avocado and pear slices. Sprinkle hemp seeds on top.

POTATO SALAD

SERVES 4 • TIME 45 MIN

6–8 large / 6 cups (750 g) potatoes chopped
1/2 tsp salt
1/8 tsp black pepper
1 stalk celery chopped
1/2 medium red pepper chopped
1/4 cup (8 g) chives finely chopped
1/2 cup (110 g) vegan mayonnaise (page 173)

1. Boil potatoes so they are cooked, but not mushy, 15–25 min.

2. Rinse with cold water. Drain and allow to cool in a mixing bowl.

3. Add salt, pepper, vegan mayonnaise, celery, red peppers and chives. Mix well.

ROASTED BUTTERCUP SQUASH SOUP
WITH CANDIED PUMPKIN SEEDS

SERVES 8 • TIME 60 MIN

1 buttercup squash
3 Tbs olive oil
2–3 medium shallots chopped
1 Tbs fresh ginger Finely chopped
4–5 cups (1000–1250 ml) veggie broth
2 stalks celery chopped
1/2 cup (100 g) maple syrup
1 Tbs chipotle powder
2 tsp chili power
1 tsp paprika
1 tsp ground cumin
1/2 tsp rubbed sage
1 Tbs hot sauce OPTIONAL

1. Preheat oven to 425° F / 220° C / Level 7.

2. Cut squash into 4 quarters, coat with 1 tablespoon of olive oil and lightly salt. Roast on baking sheet until tender, about 30 min. Remove from oven and cool.

3. Heat olive oil in large pot on medium heat. Add shallots, sauté until translucent, about 5 min. Add ginger, celery, spices and sauté another 5 min.

4. Remove skin from squash, add to pot. Stir in hot sauce, cook another 2 min.

5. Add broth. Bring to boil. Reduce heat, simmer covered 20–30 min, adding broth as desired.

6. Pour contents into blender (or use immersion blender) and blend until smooth.

CANDIED PUMPKIN SEEDS:

2 Tbs canola oil
2 Tbs brown sugar
1/2 tsp salt
1/4 cup (30 g) pumpkin seeds

1. Heat olive oil in small pan on medium heat. Stir in brown sugar. Cook 3 min.

2. Add pumpkin seeds and salt. Cook 2–3 minutes, stirring regularly. Remove from heat.

3. Pour soup into bowls, garnish with pumpkin seeds and serve.

PUMPKIN STEW

SERVES 4 • TIME 45 MIN

1 1/2 cups (300 g) **sweet seitan** chopped (page 172)
3–4 Tbs **olive oil**
1 large **onion** chopped
1 Tbs **fresh ginger** Finely chopped OPTIONAL
2 medium (180 g) **potatoes** chopped
2 stalks **celery** chopped
1 medium **carrot** chopped
4 cloves **garlic** Finely chopped
1 1/2 tsp **dried sage** ground
1 1/2 tsp **sea salt**
1 tsp **dried thyme**
2 Tbs **The Wizard's Organic Worcestershire Sauce**
2 tsp **liquid smoke**
2 cups (450 g) **pumpkin puree** (page 169)
2–3 cups (480–720 ml) **veggie broth** (page 159)
1 Tbs **fresh sage** chopped
1 Tbs **fresh parsley** chopped

1. Heat oil in large pot on medium heat. Add onions and stir for about 2 min. Add seitan and sauté until browned, about 5 min. Add ginger, potatoes, carrots, celery, garlic, sage, thyme and sea salt. Stir well.

2. Stir in Worcestershire sauce, liquid smoke, pumpkin puree. Increase heat to high.

3. Add veggie broth, stir well. Bring to boil, reduce to simmer. Cover.

4. Simmer 20 min. Remove from heat and add fresh sage and parsley.

ROASTED VEGETABLE SOUP

SERVES 6 TO 8 • TIME 60 MIN

1 cup (100 g) parsnips peeled, chopped
2 cups (200 g) potatoes peeled, chopped
1 cup (120 g) sweet potato peeled, chopped
1/2 cup (50 g) turnips chopped
1 cup (100 g) carrots chopped
4 Tbs olive oil
2 tsp dried rosemary
1 tsp dried thyme
1/2 tsp dried sage
2 leeks chopped
2 stalks celery chopped
1 Tbs apple cider vinegar
4-6 cups (1000-1450 ml) veggie broth (page 159)
1 handful kale stems Removed, chopped
1 tsp sea salt
fresh parsley chopped

1. Preheat oven to 400° F / 200° C / Level 6.

2. Chop vegetables in similar size piecces so they cook evenly.

3. In large mixing bowl, add chopped vegetables, 2 Tbs olive oil, rosemary, thyme, sage and sea salt. Toss until vegetables are evenly coated in oil and spices.

4. Spread vegetables out on a parchment paper lined baking sheet lined with parchment paper. Bake 15-20 min. Flip vegetables, roast another 15-20 min.

5. Heat 2 Tbs olive oil in large pot on medium heat. Sauté leeks until soft, about 5 min. Increase heat to high. Stir in celery and roasted vegetables. Add apple cider vinegar. Stir in veggie broth. Cover, bring to boil, reduce heat and simmer for 20 min. Remove from heat and add kale.

6. Blend with immersion blender to desired consistency, or blend until smooth in high-powered blender (e.g. Blendtec).

7. Stir in sea salt as desired. Garnish with fresh parsley.

PUMPKIN SOUP

SERVES 5 TO 6 • TIME 90 MIN

2 pie pumpkins oR **1 1/2 cups (330 g) pumpkin puree** (page 169)
I large onion chopped
4 oz (115 g) vegan cream cheese
2 Tbs vegan sour cream
3 cloves garlic chopped
3 bay leaves
1 tsp parsley
1 Tbs fresh marjoram
1/2 tsp sea salt
1/2 tsp curry powder
1/2 tsp dried sage
1/2 tsp ginger
2 stalks celery chopped
2 Tbs lime juice
2 Tbs brown sugar
3-4 cups (720-960 ml) veggie broth (page 159)
3-4 Tbs olive oil

1. Preheat oven to 450° F / 230° C / Level 8.

2. De-stem pumpkins. Carefully cut them in half. Scoop seeds out and brush olive oil on inside of pumpkin halves. Sprinkle sea salt and bake on baking sheet in oven for 40 min. When a fork goes in them easily, they're done.

3. Scoop cooked pumpkin pulp away from skin and mash in mixing bowl.

4. Heat 3 Tbs olive oil in large pot on medium heat. Add onion, sauté for 4–5 min.

5. Add celery, garlic, curry powder, sage, ginger, parsley, lime juice and sea salt. Cook for 5 min, stirring regularly. Add mashed pumpkin, veggie stock and bay leaves and increase heat to high. Bring to boil, stirring constantly, reduce heat to low. Simmer partially covered about 20 min. Remove from heat.

6. Remove the bay leaves. Carefully transfer hot liquid to blender and fill about 2/3 full. (Alternately, use an immersion blender.) Add most of fresh marjoram. Save some for garnish.

7. Add vegan cream cheese and vegan sour cream and blend until smooth.

8. Pour soup into bowls and garnish with fresh marjoram.

STARTERS
& SIDES

BRUSCHETTA

MAKES 12 TO 15 PIECES • TIME 50 MIN

4 cloves garlic
1 Tbs olive oil
4 Roma tomatoes chopped
1 red onion chopped
1 vegan baguette
6 fresh basil leaves finely chopped

1. Preheat oven to 350° F / 175° C / Level 4.

2. Slice off tops of garlic cloves. Place in tinfoil and wrap it around the garlic like a cup. Pour oil on them and close foil. Roast in oven 30–40 min.

3. Slice baguette into thin diagonal slices and place on baking sheet.
   Brush lightly with olive oil and toast in oven, 4–5 min

4. Toss tomatoes, onion and basil in a mixing bowl.

5. Mash roasted garlic in a small bowl to form paste. Spread paste on baguette slices, top with large spoonful of bruschetta mix.

CAULIFLOWER BITES

MAKES 12 TO 15 PIECES • TIME 25 MIN

1/2 head cauliflower
1 Tbs olive oil
1 tsp curry powder
1/4 tsp sea salt
1/4 tsp black pepper
1/4 tsp dried parsley
1 tsp vinegar

1. Cut cauliflower into 1/2 in (1 cm) slices.

2. Heat oil in frying pan on medium high heat. Add cauliflower, curry powder, salt, pepper, parsley and vinegar. Mix well. Reduce heat to low. Cook covered, 3–4 min.

3. Remove from heat and allow to cool.

BREADING:

1/2 cup (155 g) flour
1/2 cup (55 g) Edward & Sons Breadcrumbs
1/2 cup (120 ml) soy milk
2 tsp garlic powder
2 tsp dried parsley
2–3 Tbs canola oil

1. Prepare three separate bowls: one with flour, one with breadcrumbs, one with soy milk.

2. Add 1 tsp garlic powder and 1 tsp parsley to flour mixture, and 1 tsp garlic powder and 1 tsp parsley to breadcrumbs. Whisk both.

3. Dunk a cauliflower slice in the soy milk, then the flour, then the soymilk again and finally coat it in the bread crumb mixture. Repeat this for all of the cauliflower slices.

4. Heat canola oil in frying pan on medium high heat. Once heated, place the cauliflower slices in the pan and fry each side until golden brown, about 45 sec. Transfer from pan to paper towels to remove excess oil and all to cool.

CHEESY ZOMBIE FINGERS

MAKES 10 TO 12 STICKS • TIME 30 MIN+

2 cups (200 g) vegan cheese shreds
1 1/2 cups (175 g) Edward & Sons Breadcrumbs
5 Tbs garlic powder
1 tsp sea salt
1/2 tsp black pepper
1 Tbs dried oregano
2 cups (480 ml) soy milk
1 1/2 cups (225 g) flour
2–3 cups canola oil for frying
1/4 cup (60 g) tomato sauce (page 161)

1. Whisk garlic powder, salt, pepper and oregano in small bowl.

2. Melt cheese shreds in glass bowl in (or over) pot of boiling water, stirring regularly.

3. Add 2 tsp of garlic powder mixture and stir.

4. Pour melted cheese on a bread pan lined with parchment paper. Spread evenly. Chill in refrigerator, 60 min.

5. Carefully remove flattened cheese from pan and slice into 10 to 12 sticks, about finger width.

6. Pour breadcrumbs in bowl. Whisk remaining garlic powder mixture with breadcrumbs. Pour soy milk in separate bowl. Pour flour in another bowl.

7. Heat canola oil 2–3 in (6–8 cm) deep in saucepan on a medium heat.

8. Dunk cheese stick in soy milk, dredge it in flour, dunk it back in the soy milk, then roll it in breadcrumbs. Repeat for all cheese sticks. Carefully fry in hot oil. Once golden brown, take them out with tongs and set on paper towels.

9. Serve with tomato sauce.

BLACK BEANS

MAKES 2 CUPS • TIME 80 MIN+

1 cup (180 g) black beans
4 cups (960 ml) water
1 onion chopped
2 Tbs olive oil
1 tsp ground cumin
2 jalapenos Finely chopped
2 cloves garlic Finely chopped
2 tsp chipotle powder
2 tsp sea salt
1 Tbs hot sauce
1 Tbs lime juice

1. Soak beans for 8 hours in water. Drain and discard water.

2. Bring 4 cups water to boil in pot. Add bay leaves and soaked beans.
   Bring to boil, reduce to simmer, cover and cook 40–60 min.

3. Drain beans, remove bay leaves and save 1 cup of bean liquid and set aside.

4. Heat oil in frying pan on medium heat. Add onions and sauté 5 min.

5. Add jalapenos, chipotle powder, garlic, cumin and salt. Stir together, sauté 5 min.

6. Add hot sauce to deglaze pan.

7. Add the bean liquid and cook on medium high heat, stirring frequently until liquid is absorbed.

8. Stir in lime juice. Cover until ready to serve.

CORNBREAD

MAKES 12 TO 16 PIECES • TIME 45 MIN+

1 red pepper Finely chopped
1-2 jalapenos Finely chopped
1 large onion Finely chopped
2 Tbs olive oil

1. Heat olive oil on medium high heat in saucepan.
2. Sauté peppers and onion until lightly browned, 3–5 min. Remove from heat.

3/4 cup (115 g) stone ground corn meal
1 cup (155 g) flour
1/4 cup (60 g) cup sugar
3 tsp baking powder
1 tsp sea salt
2 Tbs chipotle pepper gRound
1 1/4 cups (300 ml) almond milk
3 Tbs canola oil

1. Preheat oven to 400° F / 200° C / Level 6.
2. In large mixing bowl, whisk together corn meal, flour, sugar, baking powder, sea salt and ground chipotle pepper.
3. Add almond milk and canola oil to dry ingredients. Mix thoroughly.
4. Grease rectangular glassware dish with oil or vegan shortening. Pour in batter.
5. Top batter with sautéed veggies and bake 20–25 min.
6. Remove from oven to cool. Cut into squares.

QUESADILLAS

SERVES 3 TO 4 • TIME 15 MIN

1 small red onion chopped
1/2 medium tomato chopped
1/2 avocado chopped
1/2 mango Finely chopped
1 Tbs lime juice
1/2 tsp sea salt

16 oz (450 g) baked tofu (page 163)
tortilla shells
2 cups (200 g) vegan cheese shreds
1 Tbs olive oil

1/2 cup (110 g) guacamole (page 71)

1. Combine onion, tomato, avocado, mango, lime juice and salt in small bowl.

2. Cut tofu into very thin slices. Arrange 4–5 slices of tofu on one half of a tortilla shell. Sprinkle vegan cheese shreds on it and top with scoop of the salsa from step 1. Fold tortilla over.

3. Heat oil in frying pan on a medium low heat. Fry quesadilla in pan on each side until golden brown, 2–3 min. Transfer to cutting board and cut into 4 triangles.

4. Serve with guacamole.

CAJUN RISOTTO BITES

SERVES 3 TO 4 • TIME 45 MIN+

3 tsp paprika
2 tsp salt
2 tsp garlic powder
1 tsp black pepper
1 tsp onion powder
1 tsp cayenne
1 tsp oregano
1 tsp thyme

4 cups (960 ml) veggie broth (page 159)
1 Tbs olive oil
1 cup (215 g) arborio rice
2 Tbs lemon juice

1 cup (115 g) Edward & Sons Breadcrumbs
1 tsp cajun seasoning
1 tsp fresh parsley chopped
1 cup (240 ml) soy milk or almond milk
3/4 cup (115 g) flour or corn starch
Canola oil for frying

1. Whisk paprika, sea salt, garlic powder, black pepper, onion powder, cayenne, oregano and thyme in small mixing bowl.

2. Bring veggie broth to boil and then remove from heat.

3. Heat oil in large saucepan on medium high heat. Add rice, stir 1 min. Add 1 cup veggie broth, cook, stirring constantly, until liquid starts to reduce. Continue to add broth slowly while stirring. Add 2 Tbs Cajun spice (from step 1) and lemon juice. Stir well. Set aside.

4. After cooled, roll rice into bite-size balls.

5. Combine breadcrumbs, cajun seasoning and parsley in a mixing bowl.

6. Set up 2 more bowls: one with soy (or almond) milk and one with flour.

7. Heat oil in fryer or medium saucepan on medium high heat.

8. Dip rice ball in soymilk, roll in flour, then dip in soymilk and lastly roll in breadcrumbs. Repeat for all rice balls.

9. Fry risotto bites in oil until golden brown, 3–5 min.

ROASTED ROSEMARY TATERS

SERVES 3 TO 4 • TIME 60 MIN

3 lbs (1.4 kg) red & white potatoes cut in quarters
2 Tbs olive oil
2 Tbs dried rosemary
1 Tbs dried thyme
1 tsp celery salt
1/4 tsp dried sage
2 tsp sea salt
1 tsp black pepper

1. Preheat oven to 400° F / 200° C / Level 6.

2. Cut potatoes to approximately same size. Add to large bowl.

3. Add oil, rosemary, thyme, celery salt, sage, salt and pepper.
   Mix until potatoes are evenly coated.

4. Pour potatoes on baking sheet, bake 35–45 min, flipping pieces over after 20 min.

SALT POTATOES

SERVES 8 TO 10 • 30 MIN

2 lbs (900 g) small potatoes
2/3 cup (200 g) salt

1/4 cup (60 g) vegan margarine
1 clove garlic Finely chopped
1 small shallot Finely chopped
fresh parsley Finely chopped

1. Boil large pot of water with potatoes and salt until easily pierced by fork, 20–25 min. Drain and discard water.

2. Melt margarine in a small pan on low heat. Add shallots and garlic, fry 5 min.

3. Transfer potatoes to serving bowl.

4. Pour margarine, shallots and garlic over potatoes. Garnish with parsley.

GUACAMOLE

MAKES ABOUT 2 CUPS • 10 MIN

2 avocados
1/2 tsp garlic powder
1 Tbs lime juice
1 small red onion chopped
1/2 jalapeno Finely chopped
1/2 tsp sea salt
1/2 tsp black pepper
1/8 tsp cayenne powder OPTIONAL

1. Slice avocados in half, remove pits and scoop into mixing bowl.
   (Save the pit to store with guac in fridge to prevent browning!)

2. Add the garlic powder, lime juice, onion, jalapeno, salt, pepper and cayenne.

3. Mash it all together.

BAKED BEANS

SERVES 6 TO 8 • TIME 2 HOURS+

2 cups (360 g) navy beans (dried)
1 tsp garlic powder
1 tsp onion powder
1 tsp chili powder
1 tsp sea salt
1/4 tsp black pepper
1/4 cup (65 g) brown sugar
1/4 cup (50 g) molasses
2 Tbs tomato paste
1 Tbs spicy brown mustard
1 tsp liquid smoke
1 cup / 7 oz (200 g) seitan (page 167) OPTIONAL

1. Add beans to large bowl of water. Soak for 8 hours or overnight.

2. Drain water, rinse beans. Add to pot of fresh water, bring to boil.

3. Add 2 Tbs sea salt to boiling water. Simmer covered, 60 min.

4. Drain the beans, but save 2 cups / 480 ml of the liquid.

5. Add to beans and saved liquid to mixing bowl.

6. Add garlic powder, onion powder, chili powder, sea salt, black pepper, sugar, molasses, tomato paste, mustard, seitan and liquid smoke. Stir all ingredients well.

7. Preheat oven to 350° F / 175° C / Level 4.

8. Pour beans into rectangular glassware dish.

9. Pour sauce over beans, distribute evenly.

10. Bake in oven for 60–90 min.

KILLER ZUCCHINI BREAD

SERVES 4 TO 6 • TIME 80 MIN

1/2 cup (115 g) vegan margarine
1 cup (235 g) sugar
2 tsp vanilla
2 Tbs almond milk or **soy milk**
1 cup (100 g) zucchini
6 oz (170 g) silken tofu
1 3/4 cup (265 g) flour
3/4 tsp baking soda
1/2 tsp baking powder
1 tsp cinnamon
1/4 tsp sea salt
1/4 cup (35 g) pecans chopped
1/4 cup (30 g) cranberries

1. In mixing bowl, add margarine which should be at room temperature and sugar. Mix together and then add vanilla and soy milk. Set aside.

2. Blend zucchini, sugar mixture and tofu in high-powered blender (e.g. Blendtec) until smooth, about 1 min. Alternately, grate zucchini and mix well in a bowl with sugar mixture and silken tofu until smooth.

3. In separate bowl, add flour, baking soda, baking powder and sea salt. Whisk together.

4. Combine all wet and dry ingredients and mix well. Add pecans and cranberries and mix a few times.

5. Preheat oven to 350° F / 175° C / Level 4.

6. Grease bread pan and pour in batter. Bake for 50–60 min. It's done when a toothpick comes out clean.

GRILLED BRUSSELS SPROUTS

SERVES 2 TO 3 • TIME 20 MIN

2 cups (200 g) Brussels sprouts
1 Tbs olive oil
1 tsp dried thyme
1 tsp dried rosemary
1 tsp sea salt
1/4 tsp black pepper
1 Tbs vegan margarine oR **olive oil**

1. Cut ends from Brussels sprouts, and then slice in half.

2. In medium mixing bowl add the Brussels sprouts, oil, thyme, rosemary, sea salt and black pepper. Toss until Brussels sprouts are evenly coated.

3. Wrap in aluminum foil or pour into metal baking pan.

4. Add margarine (or oil) and wrap foil around sprouts (or cover pan with foil).

5. Grill or roast until you can easily poke a fork into them, about 10–15 min, turning halfway through to ensure even cooking and prevent burning.

GRILLED SUMMER SQUASH SPEARS

SERVES 2 TO 3 • TIME 20 MIN

1 medium yellow squash
1 medium zucchini
1 small onion chopped
1 medium green pepper chopped
2 Tbs olive oil
1 tsp sea salt
1/4 tsp black pepper
1 tsp dried basil
1 tsp dried thyme
1 Tbs vegan margarine or **olive oil**

1. Slice yellow squash and zucchini into 4 inch long spears and add to mixing bowl. Add chopped onion and green pepper.

2. Add oil, sea salt, black pepper, basil and thyme. Toss to coat evenly.

3. Wrap in aluminum foil or pour into metal baking pan.

4. Add margarine (or oil) and seal foil (or cover pan with foil).

5. Set on hot grill for 10–15 min, shaking halfway through to ensure even cooking and prevent burning.

GRILLED ASPARAGUS

SERVES 2 TO 3 • TIME 15 MIN

1 lb (450 g) asparagus
1 tsp sea salt
1/4 tsp black pepper
1 Tbs olive oil

1. Rinse asparagus, remove rough ends.

2. In a mixing bowl, combine asparagus spears, olive oil, sea salt and pepper. Toss well to evenly coat.

3. Grill 5–7 min, turning every couple of min.

MAIN DISHES

SPICY BLACK BEAN BURGERS

MAKES 5 BURGERS • TIME 30 MIN

2 Tbs olive oil
1 large potato chopped
1 tsp dried rosemary
1 tsp dried thyme
1/2 tsp dried sage
1–3 Tbs chipotle powder
1 tsp sea salt
1 tsp pepper
1 large onion Finely chopped
2 cloves garlic Finely chopped
1 1/2 cups (250 g) black beans
1/2 poblano pepper chopped
1/4 cup (25g) grated vegan cheese OPTIONAL
2 Tbs brown sugar
2/3 to 1 cup (90 to 115 g) Edward & Sons Breadcrumbs
1/2 cup (75 g) flour
2 Tbs canola oil
1 tomato sliced
lettuce leaves for topping

1. Heat olive oil in frying pan on medium heat. Add potato, rosemary, thyme, sage, chipotle powder, sea salt and pepper. Fry 5 min.

2. Add onion, garlic and poblano pepper and stir for 5–10 min. Don't let the potatoes get too brown.

3. Remove from heat and transfer to mixing bowl.

4. Add black beans and let mixture cool down.

5. Add vegan cheese and brown sugar to mixing bowl and mash everything together with your hands. Mix in breadcrumbs until you have a firm consistency.

6. Form mixture into 3 in (8 cm) diameter patties about 3/4 in (2 cm) thick.

7. Heat canola oil in frying pan on medium heat. Coat patties in flour and place in frying pan. Cook each side until nicely browned, 4–5 min.

8. Serve on bun or bread slices, with lettuce, tomato and your choice of condiments.

CORN DOGS

MAKES 8 TO 10 CORN DOGS • TIME 25 MIN

1 cup (150 g) flour
2/3 cup (110 g) corn meal
1/4 cup (60 g) sugar
1 1/2 tsp baking powder
1/2 tsp baking soda
1 tsp sea salt
6 oz (170 g) silken tofu
1 1/4 cups (300 ml) almond milk oR **soy milk**
1 Tbs agave nectar
8–10 vegan hot dogs oR **vegan sausages**
oil foR fRying

1. In mixing bowl, add flour, corn meal, sugar, baking powder, baking soda and sea salt. Whisk together.

2. Add tofu, almond (or soy) milk and agave nectar. Mix to form a smooth batter.

3. Allow to set and chill in refrigerator for 10 min.

4. Heat canola oil in a fryer or deep pot to 350° F / 175° C medium high heat.

5. Insert skewers lengthwise in vegan hot dogs or sausages.

6. Pour batter in a tall glass. Dust vegan hot dogs with corn starch.

7. Dip in batter, coat well and carefully submerge in hot oil to fry.

8. Pull them out after they are golden brown and blot on paper towel.

NO KILLY PHILLY

MAKES 3 TO 4 SANDWICHES • TIME 30 MIN

3 cups / 20 oz (580 g) sweet seitan sliced thin (page 172)
2 Tbs olive oil
1 poblano pepper chopped
1 large onion chopped
1 Tbs The Wizard's Organic Worcestershire Sauce
3–4 vegan rolls
3–4 Tbs vegan mayonnaise (page 173)
or **BBQ sauce**

VEGAN CHEESE SAUCE:

1 cup (100 g) vegan cheese shreds
1/2 cup (120 ml) soy milk
1 tsp garlic powder
1/2 tsp chili powder
1/2 tsp paprika
1/8 tsp black pepper
1 Tbs Dijon mustard
1/4 cup (20 g) nutritional yeast flakes

1. Heat cheese shreds, soy milk, garlic powder, chili powder, paprika, pepper, nutritional yeast and mustard in a medium saucepan on medium heat. Stir frequently until everything melts together.

2. Open rolls and toast in oven, about 5 min.

3. Heat oil in frying pan on medium heat. Sauté poblano peppers and onions 4–5 min.

4. Add seitan and Worcestershire sauce and mix. Fry 3–5 min stirring frequently.

5. Spread vegan mayonnaise (or BBQ sauce) on rolls.

6. Add seitan and sautéed veggies.

7. Top with cheese sauce, close sandwich and serve.

JON'S HOMEMADE CHILI

SERVES 6 • TIME 45 MIN

3 Tbs olive oil
1 large onion chopped
1 cup (200 g) sweet seitan chopped (page 172) OPTIONAL
1 cup (100 g) raw unsalted cashews
2 cans (each 14 oz / 400 g) kidney beans
1 can (14 oz / 400 g) chickpeas
2 cans (each 14 oz / 400 g) pinto beans
2 large cans (each 28 oz / 800 g) crushed tomatoes
1 cup (240 g) brown sugar
1/4 cup (50 g) molasses
3 Tbs chili powder
2 Tbs garlic powder
3 chipotle peppers
1 tsp sea salt
1 tsp black pepper

1. Heat oil in large pot on a medium heat. Sauté onions and add cashews and seitan. Stir together.

2. Add can of kidney beans with liquid in it. Drain liquid from kidney beans and pinto beans and add to pot. Increase heat to high, stir well.

3. Add tomatoes to pot. Stir in brown sugar and molasses. Bring to simmer, reduce heat to low.

4. Stir in chili powder, garlic powder, salt and pepper.

5. Transfer approx 1 cup of liquid from pot to food processor or blender. Add the chipotle peppers and blend smooth. Add 1 tablespoon of chipotle sauce in simmering chili for mild heat. Use more as desired for spicier chili.

6. Simmer 25–30 min, stirring reguarly.

QUICHE

SERVES 6 TO 8 • TIME 90 MIN

2 1/2 cups (375 g) flour
1 tsp sea salt
1/4 tsp black pepper
1/2 tsp chili powder
1/2 tsp paprika
1 tsp dried thyme
1 cup (220 g) vegan shortening oR **margarine**
1/2 cup (110 g) vegan margarine
1/2 cup (120 ml) cold water

1. In mixing bowl, mix flour, salt, black pepper, chili powder, paprika and thyme. Add vegan margarine and shortening. Mix it in.

2. Start adding cold water 1 Tbs at a time until you get a nice flaky crust.

3. Form a ball of dough and cover with plastic wrap. Refrigerate 20 min. Roll it out between two pieces of parchment paper, about 1/4 in (1/2 cm) thick. Line it in a glass pie dish. Remove excess crust. Chill until filling is ready.

12 oz firm silken tofu
1 tsp turmeric
1 tsp garlic powder
1/4 cup (20 g) nutritional yeast flakes
1 tsp sea salt
1/8 tsp black pepper
1 tsp The Wizard's Organic Worcestershire Sauce
1 Tbs lemon juice
1/4 cup (35 g) corn starch
1/4 cup (60 ml) soy milk oR **almond milk**
1 cup (30 g) fresh spinach chopped
1/2 red pepper chopped
1 small onion chopped
4–5 strips vegan bacon oR **tempeh** chopped OPTIONAL
1 cup (100 g) vegan cheese shreds

1. In high-powered blender (e.g. Blendtec), blend tofu, turmeric, garlic powder, nutritional yeast, salt, pepper, Worcestershire sauce and lemon juice until smooth.

2. Whisk corn starch and soy milk in small bowl. Add to tofu purée and blend smooth.

3. Transfer filling to mixing bowl. Add spinach, onion, pepper, vegan bacon and 2/3 cup (65 g) vegan cheese. Mix. Pour into crust. Top with remaining vegan cheese.

4. Bake quiche at 375° F / 190° C / Level 5 for 45–50 min. Cool 10 min before cutting.

LASAGNA ROLLS

MAKES 8 ROLLS • TIME 60 MIN

8 (approx 6 oz / 170 g) lasagna noodles
1 Tbs olive oil
1 large onion chopped
16 oz (450 g) firm tofu
1 tsp salt
1 tsp black pepper
1 tsp oregano
1/2 tsp paprika
1 tsp garlic powder
2 Tbs lemon juice
1/4 cup (8 g) fresh basil chopped
1/4 cup (8 g) fresh spinach
1 tomato sliced in wedges
3/4 cup (75 g) vegan cheese shreds OPTIONAL
2 cups (480 g) tomato sauce (page 161)

1. In large pot, boil lasagna noodles 7–8 min until al dente.
   Remove from water, strain and set aside.

2. Heat oil in saucepan on medium heat. Add onions and sauté 5 min.

3. Crumble tofu into a strainer to drain excess water. Add tofu to saucepan and stir
   with onions. Mix in salt, pepper, oregano, paprika and garlic powder. Cook 5 min,
   stirring regularly.

4. Mix fresh basil into tofu mixture. Cook 1 min. Remove pan from heat.

5. Preheat oven to 350° F / 175° C / Level 4.

6. In a bread loaf pan, pour layer of tomato sauce on bottom and set aside.

7. Lay noodle flat on counter and place tofu filling on top leaving about 2 in (5 cm)
   empty at top. Layer fresh spinach onto tofu filling. Layer tomato spears on top of
   that. Top with tomato sauce and vegan cheese shreds for final layer.

8. Carefully roll up and set in pan on its side. Repeat for the rest. Pour some sauce on
   top of lasagna rolls and sprinkle more vegan cheese shreds on them.

9. Bake 20 min. Allow to cool and set a few minutes before serving.

MAC & CHEESE

SERVES 6 • TIME 45 MIN

16 oz (450 g) elbow pasta
1/4 cup (40 g) flour
1/4 cup (60 ml) canola oil
2 cups (480 ml) soy milk or almond milk
1 1/2 cups (150 g) vegan cheese shreds
2 tsp garlic powder
1 tsp dried basil
1 tsp onion powder
1/2 tsp sea salt
1/2 tsp black pepper
1/4 cup (20 g) nutritional yeast flakes OPTIONAL
1 Tbs mustard
1/4 cup (30 g) Edward & Sons Breadcrumbs
1 tsp paprika

1. Bring large pot of water to boil. Add pasta and boil for 10–12 min.

2. Preheat oven to 350° F / 175° C / Level 4.

3. Heat canola oil on medium heat in medium saucepan. Add flour and stir together to form a roux. Cook 2–3 min, stirring regularly.

4. Stir in soy milk (or almond milk). Bring to low simmer.

5. Add the vegan cheese shreds and stir again.

6. Add garlic powder, basil, onion powder, salt, pepper, mustard and nutritional yeast to cheese sauce. Stir well.

7. Strain pasta and transfer to large saucepan. Pour most of cheese sauce on the pasta and mix thoroughly.

8. Scoop noodles and cheese into glassware or casserole dish. Spread evenly.

9. Top with remaining cheese sauce and spread flat. Sprinkle breadcrumbs and dust with paprika.

10. Bake for 20–25 min until top is browned and edges are slightly crispy.

11. Allow to cool and set for 5–10 min before serving.

STUFFED SHELLS

MAKES 25 SHELLS • TIME 45 MIN

2 Tbs olive oil
1/4 cup (55 g) vegan cream cheese
1/4 cup (55 g) vegan sour cream
1 small onion chopped
1 tsp dried oregano
1 tsp dried basil
1 tsp dried thyme
1/2 tsp sea salt
1/2 tsp pepper
25 large pasta shells
1 cup (200 g) vegan meat crumbles
4–5 cups (900–1100 g) tomato sauce (page 161)
1 cup (100 g) vegan cheese shreds

1. Bring large pot of water to boil. Stir shells into water and return to boil. Cook 7–8 min, but do not overcook. Strain and rinse with cold water.

2. Preheat oven to 350° F / 175° C / Level 4.

3. Heat oil in frying pan on medium heat. Add onion and sauté 5 min.

4. Add vegan meat crumbles, sour cream and cream cheese. Stir and reduce heat to low. Stir in oregano, basil, thyme, salt and pepper. Simmer for 10 min, stirring regularly. Set aside and allow to cool.

5. Line a large glassware or baking dish with tomato sauce to cover the bottom. Carefully stuff shells with filling and arrange in dish. Cover with tomato sauce and top with vegan cheese shreds.

6. Bake 20–25 min.

CAVATELLI

SERVES 3 TO 4 • TIME 60 MIN+

12 oz (340 g) silken tofu
2 cloves garlic crushed or finely chopped
1 Tbs basil finely chopped
1 Tbs lemon juice
1 Tbs olive oil
1 tsp sea salt
2–3 cups (300–450 g) flour
2–3 cups (450–650 g) tomato sauce (page 161)

1. In mixing bowl, add tofu, garlic, basil and lemon juice. Mix until tofu is all broken up.

2. Add in oil, salt and flour. Mix together.

3. Lightly flour countertop or cutting board and knead dough until firm.

4. Wrap in shrink wrap and refrigerate 2 hours.

5. Cut into small manageable pieces and roll them out into small tubes.

6. Cut into small nuggets. Place nuggets one at a time at beginning of fork prongs and gently roll to tip of fork to form the cavatelli. (Or use cavatelli machine.)

7. Spread cavatelli pieces on baking sheet, set aside in cool, dry place 10–12 hours.

8. Bring pot of water to boil and pour in the cavatelli. Boil until they start to float to the top, about 8–10 min. Stir occasionally so they don't stick to the bottom.

9. Strain, arrange on plates and top with tomato sauce.

FETTUCCINE ALFREDO

SERVES 4 • TIME 60 MIN

3 Tbs flour
6 Tbs olive oil
1 small onion chopped
8 oz (225 g) baked tofu (page 163)
2 cups (200 g) shiitake mushrooms sliced
1/4 cup (35 g) capers
1/2 tsp sea salt
1/2 tsp black pepper
1/2 tsp dried sage
1/2 tsp dried thyme
2 cloves garlic finely chopped
2 1/2 –3 cups (600–720 ml) almond milk
1 Tbs apple cider vinegar
1 scallion chopped
16 oz (450 g) vegan fettuccine noodles

1. Heat 3 Tbs oil in large frying pan on medium heat. Add onion, mushrooms, tofu and capers. Sauté 5 min. Stir in garlic and sauté another 5 min.

2. Heat 3 Tbs oil on medium heat in separate saucepan. Add flour and stir to make a roux, about 3–4 min. Stir in almond milk, salt, pepper, sage and thyme. Increase heat to high and bring to boil while stirring frequently.

3. Remove frying pan with tofu mixture from heat and deglaze with apple cider vinegar. Put half of the mixture in a bowl and set aside. Add remaining half to the alfredo sauce. Mix well.

4. Reduce alfredo sauce to low heat and simmer until it thickens, 20–30 min.

5. Add most of chopped scallions to sauce and stir.

6. Bring pot of water to a boil for fettuccine.

7. Add fettuccine noodles to boiling pot of water. Boil until noodles are al dente – not too hard, not too soft. Remove from water and strain.

8. Scoop portion of pasta to saucepan and add desired sauce.
   Mix to cover pasta in sauce.

9. Transfer to plates and top with sautéed tofu mushroom mix and scallions.

YOU'RE MY GYRO

MAKES 4 • TIME 20 MIN

2 cups (400 g) seitan thinly sliced (page 167)
2 tsp olive oil
1 medium tomato chopped
1/2 head lettuce chopped
4 pita bread

GYRO SWEET SAUCE:
4 Tbs tahini
2 Tbs agave nectar
1/2 tsp sea salt
2 tsp fresh dill chopped
1 lemon juiced

1. Mix tahini, agave, sea salt, dill and lemon juice in a small bowl.

2. Heat olive oil in frying pan on medium heat. Fry seitan slices until slightly crispy and browned, about 1–2 min each side.

3. Spread sauce on pita bread.

4. Add seitan, tomato and lettuce and fold to close sandwich.

NEATLOAF

SERVES 3 TO 4 • TIME 60 MIN

1 cup (185 g) millet
3 medium potatoes chopped
3 medium onions finely chopped
3 cups (720 ml) veggie broth (page 159)
2 stalks celery chopped
3 cloves garlic finely chopped
1 tsp caraway seeds toasted
1 tsp dried sage
1 tsp dried thyme
1 tsp sea salt
2 Tbs balsamic vinegar
2 Tbs The Wizard's Organic Worcestershire Sauce
3 Tbs olive oil
3–4 Tbs organic ketchup

1. In medium pot bring veggie broth to boil and add the millet. Reduce heat, simmer for about 20 min until millet absorbs liquid.

2. Boil potatoes in separate pot until soft.

3. Heat olive oil in saucepan on medium high. Add onions and sauté until golden brown.

4. Add celery and garlic and sauté 2–3 min. Stir in caraway seeds, sage, thyme and sea salt. Remove from heat.

5. Add balsamic vinegar and stir a few times to deglaze.

6. In large mixing bowl, add millet, potatoes, Worcestershire sauce and sautéed onions. *Allow to cool* enough to mix together thoroughly with hands.

7. Preheat oven to 350° F / 175° C / Level 4.

8. Line loaf pan with parchment paper and pack in Neatloaf mixture well.

9. Spread ketchup evenly on top and bake 30–45 min.

10. Allow loaf to cool, remove from pan. Carefully slice with serrated knife.

CITRUS BAKED TOFU

SERVES 4 • TIME 45 MIN+

32 oz (900 g) extra firm tofu
juice of 1 orange
juice of 1 lemon
juice of 1 lime
3 Tbs agave nectar
1 Tbs fresh ginger Finely chopped
2 Tbs sugar
1 Tbs vegan margarine
2–3 Tbs canola oil
1 bunch fresh chives
1 orange sliced

1. Mix juice of orange, lemon and lime in mixing bowl.

2. Cut each tofu block into 4 equal pieces. Marinate tofu in juice for 2 hours.

3. Add marinade to saucepan and cook on high until liquid thickens enough to coat the back of a spoon. Stir in sugar and margarine.

4. Preheat oven to 375° F / 190° C / Level 5.

5. Heat oil in frying pan on high heat. Pan sear all sides of tofu pieces to seal in flavor, about 1 min each.

6. Place pieces on baking sheet, brush with sauce. Bake 15 min.

7. Flip tofu, brush with sauce and bake another 15 min.

8. Drizzle remaining sauce on plate. Arrange tofu on plate.
   Garnish with chives and fresh orange slice.

PAD THAI

SERVES 2 • TIME 30 MIN

3–4 Tbs olive oil
2 cloves garlic Finely chopped
1/2 tsp ground coriander
1/4 tsp crushed red pepper flakes
1 tsp onion powder
3 Tbs sugar
1/2 tsp apple cider vinegar
1/2 cup (100 g) baked tofu sliced (page 163)
1 1/4 cups (300 ml) veggie broth (page 159)
8 oz (225 g) rice noodles
1/4 head cabbage chopped
1 medium carrot grated or thinly sliced
4 fresh basil leaves
1/2 tsp sea salt
1 tsp The Wizard's Organic Worcestershire Sauce
1 Tbs fresh lime juice
crushed peanuts for garnish
sprouts for garnish

1. Heat olive oil in a saucepan on low heat.

2. Add garlic, coriander, crushed red pepper, sugar, onion powder and apple cider vinegar to the saucepan. Stir well.

3. Add tofu and veggie broth. Increase heat to high to reduce and thicken.

4. Boil water in pot and add rice noodles. Reduce heat, cook 5 min, stirring regularly.

5. Add cabbage and carrots to tofu pan. Stir.

6. Chiffonade (roll and thinly slice) basil and set aside for garnish.

7. With tongs, take noodles from pot and transfer directly to tofu pan. Stir.

8. Add salt, Worcestershire sauce and lime juice. Stir.

9. Transfer noodles to plates. Garnish with sprouts, crushed peanuts and basil.

POST APOCALYPTIC POT PIE

SERVES 3 TO 4 • TIME 60 MIN

2 Tbs olive oil
1 large onion chopped
2 potatoes chopped
2 cloves garlic Finely chopped
1 large carrot chopped
16 oz (450 g) baked tofu (page 163)
8 shiitake mushrooms thinly sliced OPTIONAL
2 cups (480 ml) veggie broth (page 159)
1 tsp salt
1 tsp dried thyme
1/2 tsp chili powder
1 tsp paprika
1 tsp dried parsley
2 Tbs soy sauce
2 Tbs flour

1. Heat oil in large saucepan on medium heat. Add onions. Sauté 5 min. Add potatoes, carrots, mushrooms, tofu and garlic. Mix well.

2. Add salt, pepper, thyme, chili powder, paprika, parsley, soy sauce and flour. Stir, cook 2–3 min. Stir in veggie broth. Bring to boil, cover. Reduce heat, simmer 20 min.

2 1/2 cups (375 g) flour
1 tsp sea salt
1/4 tsp black pepper
1/2 tsp chili powder
1/2 tsp paprika
1 tsp dried thyme
1 cup (220 g) vegan shortening
1/2 cup (110 g) vegan margarine
1/2 cup (120 ml) cold water

1. In mixing bowl, flour, sea salt, black pepper, chili powder, paprika, thyme and mix everything together. Add vegan margarine and shortening. Mix it in.

2. Mix in water 1 Tbs at a time until you get a nice flaky crust.

3. Transfer dough to plastic wrap and form a ball. Refrigerate for 20 min. Remove and roll it out between two pieces of parchment paper, about 1/4 in / 1/2 cm thick.

4. Preheat oven to 350° F / 175° C / Level 4.

5. Pour filling into pie or ceramic dish. Place crust over filling. Trim around edges.

6. Cut a few slices in crust to vent. Bake until crust is deep golden brown, 20–25 min.

STUFFED ACORN SQUASH

SERVES 4 • TIME 60 MIN

2 acorn squash
1 tsp sea salt
1 tsp pepper
1 medium onion chopped
1/2 cup (55 g) vegan sausage or **sweet seitan** chopped (page 172)
1/3 cup (75 g) vegan margarine
1 cup (240 ml) veggie broth (page 159)
4 cups (300 g) bread chunks
1 tsp dried thyme
1 tsp dried sage
2 Tbs olive oil
2 Tbs Edward & Sons Breadcrumbs

1. Preheat oven to 450° F / 230° C / Level 8.

2. In mixing bowl, toss chopped bread with 1 Tbs olive oil.

3. Toast bread pieces 5 min. Remove from oven, set aside.

4. Carefully cut squash in half lengthwise. Slice a small wedge off bottom so halves sit flat.

5. Brush agave nectar on each half, sprinkle with salt and pepper.

6. Bake squash 25–30 min on baking sheet.

7. Heat 1 Tbs olive oil in pan on medium heat. Sauté onion, 5 min.

8. Add vegan sausage (or seitan) and sauté another 2–3 min. Remove from heat.

9. In medium pot, bring veggie broth to boil. Add margarine and stir. Turn heat off and add chopped bread, thyme and sage. Stir in sautéed vegan sausage and onions.

10. Remove squash from oven and fill each one with the stuffing.

11. Top with breadcrumbs.

12. Bake another 20–25 min.

STUFFED PEPPER HALVES

MAKES 6 • TIME 60 MIN

RICE FILLING:
1/2 cup (105 g) brown rice
1 1/4 cups (300 ml) water
1 tsp garlic powder
1 tsp chili powder
1 tsp paprika
1/2 tsp ground cumin
1/8 tsp black pepper
1/8 tsp sea salt
1/4 cup (25 g) vegan cheese shreds

BEAN FILLING:
2 Tbs olive oil
1 medium onion chopped
1 cup (160 g) black beans
2 cloves garlic crushed or finely chopped
1 chipotle pepper chopped OPTIONAL
3 small sweet peppers finely chopped
1/2 cup (55 g) frozen corn
1 tsp chili powder
1 tsp paprika
1/2 tsp sea salt

3 poblano peppers or **green peppers**
2 Tbs Edward & Sons Breadcrumbs

1. Rice Filling: In medium saucepan bring water to boil. Stir in rice, cover and reduce heat to low. Cook until rice is done. Remove from heat.

2. Stir in garlic powder, chili powder, paprika, cumin, salt, pepper and cheese shreds.

3. Bean Filling: Heat oil on medium heat in frying pan. Add onions, sauté 3 min. Stir in beans and garlic. Add desired amount of chipotle pepper. Add sweet peppers and corn. Stir in chili powder, paprika, sea salt. Simmer on medium low heat, 10–15 min.

4. Preheat oven to 350° F / 175° C / Level 4.

5. Slice peppers in half lengthwise and scoop out seeds.

6. Scoop rice filling into pepper halves. Top with bean filling. Top with breadcrumbs.

7. Place on baking sheet and bake 25 min.

SHEPHERD'S PIE

SERVES 3 TO 4 • TIME 60 MIN+

POTATO TOPPING:

2 cups (200 g) potatoes chopped
1 cup (100 g) sweet potatoes chopped
1 Tbs vegan margarine
1/4 tsp pepper
1/2 tsp sea salt
1/4 cup (20 g) nutritional yeast flakes

1. Boil potatoes in large pot until soft, 20–25 min.
2. Strain potatoes and add to mixing bowl. Add margarine, salt, pepper and nutritional yeast. Mash well.

PIE FILLING:

1 Tbs olive oil
1/2 cup (60 g) shallot chopped
1/2 cup (60 g) celery chopped
1/2 cup (60 g) carrots chopped
1 1/2 cups (300 g) sweet seitan chopped (page 172)
1 Tbs olive oil
1 Tbs flour
1 tsp apple cider vinegar
1 cup (240 ml) veggie broth
1 tsp garlic powder
1/2 tsp sea salt
1/4 tsp pepper
1/2 tsp thyme

1. Heat oil in pot on medium heat. Add shallots and sauté about 5 min, stirring occasionally. Add celery, carrots and seitan. Cook 5 min, stirring often.
2. Push contents of pot to one side and on empty side add flour and olive oil and stir to form a roux. Then mix together and deglaze with vinegar. Stir.
3. Preheat oven to 350° F / 175° C / Level 4.
4. Add veggie broth to pot and increase heat to high. Add garlic powder, salt, pepper and thyme. Stir. Cover and cook 10 min.
5. Add filling to a pie dish (or all stainless steel frying pan) Spread out evenly.
6. Add potato topping, spread evenly. Make a few slices in middle for air to escape.
7. Bake 45 min. Allow to cool and set briefly before serving.

TWICE BAKED SWEET POTATOES

SERVES 2 TO 3 • TIME 80 MIN

3 large sweet potatoes
2 Tbs vegan margarine
1 Tbs vegan sour cream
1/4–1/2 cup (60–120 ml) soy milk
1/2 cup (50 g) vegan cheese shreds
4 Tbs vegan parmesan cheese
1/2 tsp dried sage
1/2 tsp onion powder
1 tsp sea salt
1/2 tsp pepper
3–4 Tbs coconut bacon bits (page 165)

1. Preheat oven to 450° F / 230° C / Level 8.

2. Poke holes in sweet potatoes with fork, wrap in tinfoil and bake 40 min. (Leave oven on for second baking.)

3. Cut potatoes in half lengthwise. Scoop out inside of potatoes leaving about 1/2 in (1 cm) border.

4. Mash potato filling in a bowl. Add soy milk, vegan sour cream, vegan butter, vegan cheese shreds, vegan parmesan cheese, sage, onion powder, and salt. Stir everything together.

5. Scoop filling into sweet potato halves. Sprinkle vegan cheese shreds and pepper on each half.

6. Place potatoes on baking sheet and bake 20 min.

7. Plate potatoes and sprinkle coconut bacon bits on top.

TAMALES

MAKES 15 TAMALES • TIME 90 MIN

    corn husks
    1 Tbs olive oil
    1 medium onion chopped
    8 cloves garlic crushed or finely chopped
    1 1/2 tsp chili powder
    1 cup (110 g) vegan meat crumbles
    2 cups (320 g) cooked black beans
    1 tsp sea salt
    1 tsp black pepper
    1 Tbs apple cider vinegar

1. Soak corn husks in hot water 60 min.

2. Bean mix: Heat oil in saucepan on medium heat. Add garlic, onion and chili powder. Sauté 5 min, stirring occasionally. Add meat crumbles and stir. Add black beans, salt, pepper and apple cider vinegar. Stir together, cook 5 min. Remove from heat.

3. Blend or thoroughly mash bean mixture, then transfer to a bowl.

DOUGH MIX:

    3 1/4 cups (500 g) masa corn flour
    3 cups (720 ml) veggie broth (page 159)
    1/2 cup (120 ml) canola oil
    1/2 tsp baking powder
    1 tsp sea salt
    1 Tbs agave nectar
    1 Tbs chili powder

1. In mixing bowl, add masa, veggie broth, canola oil, baking powder, sea salt, agave nectar and chili powder. Mix until it forms a ball of dough. Set aside.

2. Flatten a corn husk out on counter. Take small amount of dough, about 3–4 Tbs, and center it on corn husk. Flatten it out to 1/4 in (1/2 cm) thick.

3. Add a strip of 2–3 Tbs bean mixture to flattened dough and fold husk around it to cover the bean mixture.

4. Put tamales in a steamer and steam about 60 min.

5. Remove corn husk and use red sauce to dip tamales in.

TEMPEH LETTUCE TOMATO

MAKES 3 TO 4 SANDWICHES • TIME 25 MIN

12–16 slices tempeh bacon (page 36)
1 Tbs olive oil
6–8 slices bread
1/2 head lettuce
1 tomato sliced
vegan mayonnaise (page 173)
avocado sliced OPTIONAL
pinch sea salt

1. Heat 1 Tbs olive oil in a frying pan on medium heat. Fry tempeh slices on both sides until crispy, 3–4 min.

2. Toast bread and spread vegan mayonnaise on both slices.

3. Add lettuce, two slices of tomato, avocado, salt and 3–4 slices of tempeh bacon. Top with other bread slice. Cut sandwich in halves and serve.

PIZZA

SERVES 3 TO 4 • TIME 30 MIN

1 pizza dough (page 175)
1 cup (225 g) tomato sauce (page 161)
1/2 fresh red pepper chopped
8-10 basil leaves freshly chopped
1 Tbs olive oil
2 cups (200 g) vegan cheese shreds
1 tsp garlic powder
1 tsp dried parsley
1/2 tsp dried oregano

1. Form dough into a pizza shell and place on pizza tray.

2. Preheat oven to 425° F / 220° C / Level 7.

3. Add sauce to middle of pizza shell and work it out in a spiral motion towards the edges with a ladle.

4. In mixing bowl, add vegan cheese shreds, chopped basil and chopped red pepper. Mix together and then sprinkle on pizza evenly.

5. In small bowl, mix garlic powder, parsley and oregano. Sprinkle on pizza.

6. Brush olive oil on the crust and bake until bottom in nicely browned, 10–12 min.

7. Remove from oven and slice into 6 to 8 pieces

BROCCOLI & SPINACH STUFFED PIZZA

SERVES 4 TO 6 • TIME 30 MIN

2 pizza doughs (page 175)
2 cups (60 g) fresh baby spinach
2 cups (110 g) fresh broccoli chopped
2 cloves garlic crushed or finely chopped
1/2 cup / 4 oz (115 g) vegan cream cheese OPTIONAL
1 cup (225 g) tomato sauce (page 161)
2 cups (200 g) vegan cheese shreds OPTIONAL
1 tsp garlic powder
1/2 tsp parsley
1/2 tsp oregano

1. Preheat oven to 425° F / 220° C / Level 7.

2. Steam broccoli and spinach until tender, 8–10 min.

3. Stretch both pizza dough shells out.

4. Place one crust on lightly oiled pizza pan. This is your bottom crust.

5. Spread vegan cream cheese on bottom crust. Add tomato sauce and spread out in spiral motion from center to edge. Add steamed veggies and spread evenly. Add garlic. Add vegan cheese shreds.

6. Cover pizza with the second crust. Fold lip over tightly making sure no sauce gets on the edge. Using a hard object – such as wooden spoon handle – pinch down around lip of pizza and trim excess dough off.

7. In small bowl, mix 2 Tbs olive oil with 1 Tbs tomato sauce. Brush over top of pizza.

8. Cut 2 or 3 slits in top shell.

9. In small bowl, combine garlic powder, parsley and oregano. Sprinkle over pizza.

10. Bake pizza until bottom is golden brown, 10–15 mins.

11. Remove from oven. Allow to cool 5 min before slicing.

PIZZA ROLLS

MAKES 4 TO 6 ROLLS • TIME 35 MIN

2 cups (200 g) Seitan or **baked tofu** (page 167 or 163)
2 vegan sausages OPTIONAL
2 cups (200 g) vegan cheese shreds
1 cup tomato sauce (page 161)
1 medium onion chopped
1/4 cup (30 g) fresh basil chopped
2 Tbs olive oil

1. Preheat oven to 425° F / 220° C / Level 7.

2. Roll out dough on counter to form a large circle. Use pizza cutter to cut dough in half twice (into quarters) forming large triangles. Cut in 1/8ths to make smaller rolls, if preferred.

3. With spoon, form a line of tomato sauce about 1 inch from the outer lip of each dough triangle. Do not get sauce on the corners. Next place vegan sausage, seitan (or tofu) on the line of sauce. Add fresh basil and onion. Top with cheese shreds.

4. Take left and right corners of the dough and fold them up and over and stick them near the center of triangle. Carefully fold outer lip of dough over filling and roll it up. Repeat for each pizza roll.

5. Place pizza rolls on baking sheet.

6. In small bowl, mix olive oil and 2 Tbs tomato sauce. Brush on top of the uncooked pizza rolls.

7. Bake pizza rolls in oven until golden brown, about 15–20 min.

SEITAN MUSHROOM MEATBALLS

MAKES 8 TO 10 MEATBALLS • TIME 45 MIN

1 cup / 7 oz (200 g) seitan chopped (page 167)
1 cup (90 g) shiitake mushrooms chopped
2 large shallots chopped
1 clove garlic Finely chopped
1 tsp paprika
2 tsp dried oregano
1/2 tsp cayenne pepper
1 tsp sea salt
1/2 tsp black pepper
3 Tbs olive oil
1–2 Tbs Edward & Sons Breadcrumbs (as needed)

1. Heat 2 Tbs olive oil in frying pan on medium heat. Add shallots and cook for 2 min. Add mushrooms and seitan and cook for 5 min. Add garlic, paprika, oregano, cayenne, salt and pepper. Cook 3–5 min.

2. Add everything to food processor and chop into small pieces, about 1 min. Add 1 Tbs olive oil if mixture is too dry. Alternately, add breadcrumbs if mixture is too wet and doesn't stick together well.

3. Preheat oven to 350° F / 175° C / Level 4.

4. Roll mixture into 2 in (5 cm) balls.

5. Bake 20 min, turning once.

6. Remove from heat. Serve with your favorite pasta and sauce.

TEMPEH KABOBS

MAKES 6 TO 8 KABOBS • TIME 60 MIN

4 cups (960 ml) veggie broth
1 tsp sea salt
1 tsp chili powder
1 tsp mesquite powder
2 Tbs Dijon mustard or spicy brown mustard
2 Tbs olive oil
1 chipotle pepper
2 Tbs The Wizard's Organic Worcestershire Sauce
2 Tbs agave nectar
8 oz (225 g) tempeh
juice of 1/2 lime
2 Tbs fresh parsley Finely chopped
1/2 cup (80 g) cremini mushrooms
8–10 cherry tomatoes
1 green pepper chopped
1 large onion chopped
1 cup (100 g) seitan chopped OPTIONAL
BBQ sauce OPTIONAL

1. Heat medium saucepan to high heat. Add veggie broth, sea salt, chili powder, mesquite, mustard, olive oil, chipotle pepper, Worcestershire sauce and agave. Whisk it all together and bring to a boil.

2. Cut tempeh into 1 inch (2 cm) cubes and add to saucepan marinade. Cover and reduce to simmer for 20 min. Remove from heat.

3. Add lime juice and parsley to marinade. Whisk it together. Add mushrooms, tomatoes, pepper and onion to marinade and let sit 20 min.

4. Soak wooden skewers and then assemble kabobs however you please. Brush with BBQ sauce. Set them on grill and let them brown, turning them as they cook.

5. Add salt to taste.

DESSERTS & DRINKS

CHOCOLATE MOUSSE

SERVES 2 TO 3 • TIME 30 MIN

1 can (14 oz / 400 ml) coconut milk
1 Tbs agar-agar
1/4 cup (50 g) agave nectar
1/3 cup (55 g) semi-sweet chocolate chips
1 pinch sea salt
1 pinch cayenne
4–6 strawberries sliced

1. Bring coconut milk to boil in medium saucepan.

2. Add agar-agar and agave. Reduce heat. Simmer 5–10 min, stirring occasionally.

3. Strain coconut milk mixture and pour it back in saucepan. Return to simmer.

4. Stir in chocolate chips, sea salt and cayenne.

5. Stir continuously until chocolate chips are melted.

6. Pour into bowl and set in refrigerator.

NUT CRUST:

1/2 cup (80 g) almonds lightly roasted
1 pinch sea salt
1 tsp agave nectar

1. Pulse almonds, sea salt and agave a few times in food processor until almonds are coarsely chopped.

2. Place chopped almonds in bottom of serving dish(es).

3. Remove chilled mousse from refrigerator and mix in food processor until smooth and creamy consistency.

4. Pour mousse in serving dish(es) over almonds and garnish with sliced strawberries.

PEACH PERFECTION

SERVES 4 • TIME 45 MIN+

4 peaches
4 Tbs lemon juice
1/4 tsp sea salt
1 cup (120 g) cashews
2 Tbs coconut oil
1 tsp agave nectar
1/4 cup (35 g) pumpkin seeds
2 Tbs canola oil
2 Tbs brown sugar
1/8 tsp cinnamon

1. Soak cashews in water 8 hours or overnight. Drain and discard water.

2. Preheat oven to 425° F / 220° C / Level 7.

3. Toss peach halves in lemon juice and salt. Place on baking sheet and roast 25 min. Remove from oven and set aside.

4. Blend cashews, coconut oil and agave in high-powered blender (e.g. Blendtec) until smooth, about 1 min.

CANDIED PUMPKIN SEEDS:

2 Tbs canola oil
2 Tbs brown sugar
1/2 tsp salt
1/4 cup (35 g) pumpkin seeds

1. Heat oil in small saucepan on medium heat and stir in brown sugar. Cook 2–3 min, stirring regularly.

2. Add pumpkin seeds and salt. Cook another 2–3 min. Remove from heat.

3. Fill peaches with cashew cream, top with candied pumpkin seeds and dust with cinnamon.

RAW BLUEBERRY CHEESECAKE

MAKES 2 SMALL CAKES • TIME 60 MIN+

2 cups (250 g) raw cashews
1/2 cup (95 g) blueberries
1/4 cup (50 g) agave nectar
1/4 cup (35 g) macadamia nuts
1/4 cup (35 g) walnuts
1 Tbs extra virgin coconut oil
2 dates (pitted)
1 pinch sea salt
8–12 strawberries

1. Soak cashews in water 8 hours or overnight. Drain and discard water.

2. Blend cashews, blueberries and agave in high-powered blender (e.g. Blendtec) until smooth, thick consistency, about 60–90 sec.

3. Pulse macadamia nuts, walnuts, coconut oil, dates and salt in food processor to a rough chop, so mixture sticks together.

4. Coat two 5 in (13 cm) spring molds with coconut oil and pack bottoms with the sticky date nut crust.

5. Add blueberry mixture. Place parchment paper over top. Secure with rubber band.

6. Place in freezer for 6–8 hours, then transfer to refrigerator.

7. Decorate top with strawberries (or other fruit).

CHOCOLATE WACKY CAKE

SERVES 6 TO 8 • TIME 60 MIN.

WACKY CAKE:
1 1/2 cups (225 g) flour
1 tsp baking soda
1 tsp sea salt
1 cup (235 g) sugar
1/3 cup (30 g) cocoa powder
1 Tbs vinegar
5 Tbs canola oil
1 tsp vanilla
1 cup (240 ml) warm water

1. Preheat oven to 350° F / 175° C / Level 4.
2. In mixing bowl, whisk flour, baking soda, salt, sugar and cocoa powder.
3. In separate mixing bowl, whisk vinegar, oil, warm water and vanilla.
4. Pour the wet ingredients into dry mixture. Stir until batter is smooth.
5. Lightly coat cake tin with canola oil. Dust with cocoa powder so it sticks to sides and bottom.
6. Pour cake batter in cake tin and spread evenly.
7. Bake 20–25 min. Allow to cool before frosting.

FROSTING:
1/3 cup (75 g) vegan margarine
1/3 cup (75 g) vegan shortening
1 Tbs agave nectar
1/2 cup (120 g) creamy peanut butter
1 cup (160 g) powdered sugar

1. Whip margarine and shortening in mixing bowl.
2. Stir in agave and peanut butter.
3. Gradually add powdered sugar, 1/4 cup at a time. Mix until smooth.
4. Frost cake after it has cooled.

BROWNIES

MAKES 9 BROWNIES • TIME 60 MIN

1/4 cup (55 g) vegan margarine
1/4 cup (55 g) vegan shortening
1 cup (235 g) sugar
1/2 tsp baking powder
1/4 tsp sea salt
1/2 cup (45 g) cocoa powder
3/4 cup / 6 oz (170 g) silken tofu
1 tsp vanilla extract
1/4 cup (60 ml) almond milk
1 Tbs peanut butter OPTIONAL
2/3 cup (100 g) flour
1/4 cup (45 g) agave nectar
1/4 cup / 1.5 oz (40 g) chocolate chips OPTIONAL

1. Preheat oven to 350° F / 175° C / Level 4.

2. In mixing bowl, add room temperature margarine and shortening and mix with fork.

3. Add sugar, baking powder, sea salt, cocoa powder and tofu. Mix well.

4. Add vanilla extract, almond milk, agave nectar and peanut butter. Mix well.

5. Add flour and stir in chocolate chips.

6. Line medium size (8 x 8 in / 20 x 20 cm) glassware dish with parchment paper and pour in batter. Spread evenly.

7. Bake 35–45 min. When a toothpick comes out clean, the brownies are done.

AUTUMN SPICE POACHED PEARS

MAKES 4 TO 6 • TIME 60 MIN+

4 to 6 ripe pears
4 cups (960 ml) apple cider (non-alcoholic)
1 Tbs cinnamon
3/4 tsp ground cloves
1 tsp ground nutmeg

1. Add all ingredients to large saucepan and bring to boil.
2. Reduce heat to low simmer.
3. Add pears and cook until tender, about 20 min.
4. Remove from liquid and set aside.

BERRY COULIS:

1/4 cup (50 g) blackberries
1/4 cup (50 g) blueberries
1/2 tsp sea salt
1/4 cup (60 ml) water
1/4 cup (60 g) sugar
1/4 tsp cayenne

1. Add coulis ingredients to small saucepan on medium heat. Stir regularly until fruit breaks down, about 10 min.
2. Remove from heat and blend until smooth.

1 roll phyllo dough
2 Tbs canola oil
2 mint leaves chiffonade or chopped
blackberries for garnish
cinnamon for garnish

1. Preheat oven to 350° F / 175° C / Level 4.
2. For each pear, lay down a sheet of phyllo dough and set pear on it. Wrap sheet around pear and brush with oil. Repeat, using 4 to 5 sheets of phyllo for each pear.
3. Place pears on baking sheet. Bake until golden brown, 15–20 min.
4. Drizzle plate with coulis and place pear on top.
5. Garnish with blackberry and fresh mint. Dust with cinnamon.

PEANUT BUTTER CHOCOLATE CHIP COOKIES

MAKES ABOUT 20 COOKIES • TIME 30 MIN

3/4 cups (180 g) creamy peanut butter
1/3 cup (75 g) vegan margarine
3/4 cup (180 g) sugar
1/2 cup (120 ml) almond milk
1/2 tsp vanilla extract
1/4 tsp salt
1 tsp baking powder
2 cups (300 g) flour
1/2 cup (85 g) chocolate chips

1. Preheat oven to 350° F / 175° C / Level 4.

2. In mixing bowl, combine vegan margarine, peanut butter and sugar.

3. Stir in vanilla extract and almond milk.

4. Add sea salt, baking powder and flour. Mix well.

5. Mix in chocolate chips.

6. Scoop out 1 Tbs cookie dough and roll it into a ball. Roll in sugar and place on baking tray lined with parchment paper. Repeat.

7. Bake until light golden brown, about 10–12 min.

8. Remove from oven and flatten each cookie with fork and allow to cool down.

S'MORES KRISPY TREATS

MAKES 9 SQUARES • TIME 15 MIN

10 oz (280 g) vegan marshmallows
3 Tbs vegan margarine
2 cups vegan graham crackers crumbled
3 cups crisp rice cereal
2 Tbs agave nectar
3–4 Tbs / 1.5 oz (40 g) vegan chocolate chips

1. Melt margarine in large pot on medium heat.

2. Add agave nectar. Add marshmallows and crumbled graham crackers, but save a handful of each for topping.

3. Stir until everything is melted together. Remove from heat.

4. Add crisp rice cereal. Mix well.

5. Pour mixture into 8 x 8 in (20 x 20 cm) glassware dish. Spread evenly.

6. Top with marshmallows and crumbled graham crackers.

7. Melt chocolate chips in double boiler. Drizzle over krispy treats.

8. Allow to cool a few minutes. Cut into squares.

VEGAN SOFT SERVE ICE CREAM

SERVES 3 TO 4 • TIME 15 MIN+

5–6 frozen bananas
1 1/2 cups (360 ml) chocolate almond milk
2 Tbs cacao powder OPTIONAL
1/4 tsp cinnamon
2 Tbs almond butter
2 fresh mint leaves
1 tsp maca powder OPTIONAL

1. Peel bananas and freeze 8 hours, or overnight. Ripe bananas are best!

2. Place frozen bananas, almond milk, cacao powder, cinnamon, almond butter and fresh mint in high-powered blender (e.g. Blendtec).

3. Blend until smooth, about 60 sec.

4. Scoop into bowls and garnish with mint leaf, if desired.

PUMPKIN ROLL

SERVES 6 • TIME 60 MIN+

1 cup (235 g) sugar
2/3 cup (145 g) pumpkin puree (page 169)
1 1/2 Tbs egg replacer or **corn starch**
6 Tbs (90 ml) water
3/4 cup (115 g) flour
1 tsp baking powder
1 tsp lemon juice
1 tsp cinnamon
1/8 tsp ground nutmeg

1. Preheat oven to 350° F / 175° C / Level 4.

2. Thoroughly mix egg replacer (or corn starch) and water in mixing bowl.

3. Add pumpkin purée. Stir together and add sugar, lemon juice, baking powder, cinnamon and nutmeg. Mix everything and gradually stir in flour.

4. Line baking sheet with parchment paper. Spray paper with nonstick spray.

5. Pour pumpkin batter on parchment and spread as smooth and even as possible. Bake 15 min. When it bounces back when pushed down on, it's done.

FILLING:

8 oz (225 g) vegan cream cheese
1/4 cup (55 g) vegan margarine
1 cup (155 g) powdered sugar
1/4 tsp vanilla extract

1. Let margarine and cream cheese warm to room temperature in mixing bowl, about 60 min. Add vanilla. Add sugar slowly, while stirring. Put bowl in refrigerator.

2. Lay a smooth sheet or towel on counter and sprinkle powdered sugar on it. Carefully take parchment sheet of pumpkin layer and flip over onto sheet. Sprinkle some more powdered sugar on the pumpkin layer.

3. Carefully roll sheet with pumpkin layer into a cylinder and refrigerate 1 hour.

4. Pull pumpkin roll out and unroll it on counter. Spread cream cheese filling evenly on surface of pumpkin sheet leaving 2 in (5 cm) unfrosted at the top. Begin to roll the pumpkin layer up starting closest to you and ending furthest from you. Do not roll the towel this time.

5. Place in freezer for about 1 hour. Remove and slice.

PUMPKIN MUFFINS

MAKES 6 • TIME 30 MIN

1 1/2 cups (225 g) flour
1 tsp cinnamon
1/2 tsp sea salt
1/2 tsp ground nutmeg
1 1/2 tsp baking powder
1 tsp baking soda
3/4 cup (165 g) pumpkin puree (page 169)
1/2 cup (100 g) pure maple syrup
1/3 cup (80 ml) coconut oil (refined)
1 tsp apple cider vinegar
1/2 cup (120 ml) apple cider (non alcoholic)
6 dates chopped

1. Preheat oven to 350° F / 175° C / Level 4.

2. Whisk flour, cinnamon, salt, nutmeg, baking powder and baking soda in mixing bowl.

3. In separate mixing bowl, mix pumpkin puree, maple syrup, melted coconut oil, apple cider vinegar and apple cider.

4. Pour wet ingredients into dry ingredients and mix gently.

5. Add chopped dates to batter. Stir in a few times.

6. Lightly coat muffin pan with coconut oil. Scoop batter in tin for each muffin to make 6 jumbo muffins.

7. Bake 20 min.

CARROT CAKE CUPCAKES

created by Sugar Mamas

MAKES 12 CUPCAKES • TIME 50 MIN

2/3 cup (100 g) flour
3/4 tsp baking soda
1/4 tsp baking powder
1/4 tsp salt
1/4 tsp cinnamon
1/4 tsp ground nutmeg
1/4 tsp allspice
1/4 tsp ground ginger
1/4 tsp ground cloves
1/3 cup (80 ml) canola oil
1/3 cup (75 g) vanilla soy yogurt
1/3 cup (75 g) pumpkin puree (page 169)
2/3 cup (155 g) sugar
1 tsp vanilla extract
1 cup (100 g) carrots grated
1/4 cup (30 g) raisins

1. In a mixing bowl, whisk flour, baking soda, baking powder, sea salt, cinnamon, nutmeg, allspice, ginger and cloves.

2. In mixing bowl (or mixer) add oil, soy yogurt, pumpkin puree, sugar and vanilla. Mix together and slowly add in dry ingredients. Do not over mix or cupcakes will be too dense. Stir in carrots and raisins.

3. Spray cupcake liners with canola oil. Fill liners about 2/3 full with batter.

4. Preheat oven to 350° F / 175° C / Level 4.

5. Bake 25 min, or until a toothpick comes out clean. Allow to cool before frosting.

MAPLE CINNAMON FROSTING:

1/2 cup (110 g) vegan shortening
1/2 cup (110 g) vegan margarine
2 Tbs soy milk or almond milk
3-4 Tbs maple syrup
4 cups (400 g) powdered sugar

1. In mixing bowl add shortening and margarine. Mix until fluffy. Add soy milk and maple syrup. Slowly mix in powdered sugar until you get desired consistency

2. Scoop frosting into frosting bag and frost cupcakes ,or use a knife to frost them.

3. Lightly dust cupcakes with cinnamon.

GINGERBREAD COOKIES

MAKES 15 TO 20 COOKIES • TIME 45 MIN

1/2 cup (110 g) vegan margarine
1/2 cup (90 g) maple syrup
1/2 cup (90 g) molasses
1 tsp cinnamon
1 tsp ginger
1 tsp all spice
1/2 tsp ground cloves
1 tsp baking soda
1 tsp vinegar
2 1/2 cups (375 g) flour

1. In mixing bowl add room temperature vegan margarine, maple syrup, molasses and vinegar. Mix it all together.

2. In separate mixing bowl, add baking soda, cinnamon, ginger, all spice, cloves, baking soda and flour. Whisk it all together.

3. Add wet ingredients to dry ingredients. Mix together until it forms a dough ball. If dough is too wet add about 1/4 cup of flour. Transfer to plastic baggie and refrigerate at least 1 hour.

4. Remove from refrigerator and put dough on parchment paper. Roll it out with rolling pin, about 1/4 in / 1/2 cm thick.

5. Preheat oven to 375° F / 190° C / Level 5.

6. Use cookie cutters to shape cookies. Place on cookie sheet lined with parchment paper. Bake 5 min.

7. Remove from oven and cool before frosting.

ICING

2 Tbs vegan margarine
2 Tbs vegan shortening
1 tsp vanilla extract
1–1 1/2 cup (155–230 g) powdered sugar

1. Add margarine, shortening and vanilla extract to mixing bowl. Mix it together.

2. Mix in 1/2 cup powdered sugar. Continue adding sugar until icing becomes stiff.

3. Fill frosting bag with icing. Alternately, use a plastic baggie: Cut a small hole in the corner of bag. Squeeze icing onto cookie and decorate – or use knife to spread icing on cookies.

CHOCOLATE PUDDING

SERVES 2 TO 4 • TIME 15 MIN+

1/4 cup (50 g) maple syrup
1/2 cup (95 g) raspberries
1/3 cup (30 g) cocoa powder
1/4 cup (40 g) corn starch
1 cup (235 g) sugar
3 cups (720 ml) soy milk
3–4 Tbs cup vegan cookie crumbs
fresh mint leaves

1. Heat maple syrup and raspberries in small pot on medium heat. Using wooden spoon, break up raspberries while stirring, about 10 min. Remove from heat and strain through colander and cool in refrigerator.

2. Heat soy milk on medium heat in medium saucepan. Whisk in cocoa powder, corn starch and sugar, stirring until it thickens. Remove from heat, transfer to bowl.

3. In margarita glass or small bowls, put cookie crumbs in bottom. Top with pudding.

4. Drizzle raspberry sauce over pudding. Top with with cookie crumbles.

5. Chill in refrigerator for 1+ hour. Garnish with a mint leaf.

BERRY SMOOTHIE

SERVES 2 • TIME 5 MIN
16 oz (480 ml) young coconut water
1 cup (180 g) frozen peaches
1 cup (180 g) frozen mango
1 1/2 cups (140 g) frozen mixed berries (strawberries, raspberries & blueberries)

1. Blend all ingredients in high-powered blender (e.g. Blendtec) for 30 sec.

2. Garnish with berries or fresh mint leaves if desired.

PROTEIN SHAKE

MAKES 2+ CUPS • TIME 5 MIN
1 1/2 cups (360 ml) chocolate almond milk
2 large frozen bananas
1 Tbs hemp seeds
2 tsp flax seeds ground
2 Tbs almond butter
1 tsp cinnamon
2 ripe Medjool dates (pitted)
2 Tbs protein powder

1. Blend all ingredients in high-powered blender (e.g. Blendtec) for 30 sec.

2. Pour into a large glass.

BASICS
& BEYOND

VEGGIE BROTH

MAKES ABOUT 5 QUARTS / 5 L • TIME 2 HOURS

4 onions chopped
2 carrots chopped
2–3 stalks celery chopped
1 bunch fresh parsley chopped
7 cloves garlic crushed or chopped
2 Tbs thyme
5–6 bay leaves
3 Tbs olive oil
6 quarts (6 L) water

1. In large pot, heat olive oil on medium heat. Add onions and sauté for 4 to 5 min. Turn heat to high and add carrots, celery, parsley, thyme, garlic and bay leaves. Stir together and let cook for about 5 min.

2. Add water to pot and bring to a boil. Once it starts boiling, turn it down to medium heat, cover and let cook for 60–90 min.

3. Fill sink with cold water and ice. Take pot of veggie broth from stove and put in ice water to cool off.

4. Line colander with cheese cloth and place over separate large pot. Take cooled pot of veggie broth and strain it through the cheese cloth.

5. Broth can be frozen for up to 3 months… or used immediately.

TOMATO SAUCE

MAKES 4 CUPS • TIME 45 MIN

12 Roma tomatoes
1 Tbs olive oil
3 cloves garlic crushed or finely chopped
1 tsp dried basil
1 tsp dried oregano
1/4 tsp crushed red pepper
1/4 tsp black pepper
1 tsp agave nectar OPTIONAL
1 tsp sea salt

1. Quarter tomatoes, remove seeds and place in strainer to strain the juice.
   Dice up rest of tomatoes.

2. Heat oil in saucepan on medium heat. Add garlic and stir. Add chopped tomatoes.
   Increase heat to medium high and add the strained juice.

3. Add basil, oregano, crushed red pepper, black pepper and agave.
   Bring to slow boil, reduce heat and simmer 20 min.

4. Add salt to taste.

BAKED TOFU

MAKES 16 OZ / 450 G • TIME 60 MIN+

16 oz (450 g) extra firm tofu
2 cups (480 ml) veggie broth (page 159)
1 small onion chopped
2 cloves garlic crushed or finely chopped
1 Tbs sugar
2 tsp liquid smoke
1 tsp sea salt
1 Tbs olive oil

1. Wrap tofu in paper towel or clean dish towel and place a pan or heavy cutting board on top for at least 15 min to press out excess moisture.

2. For the marinade: Mix veggie broth, onion, garlic, sugar, liquid smoke, sea salt and olive oil in mixing bowl.

3. Cut tofu in half and place in marinade. Cover, refrigerate overnight.

4. Preheat oven to 350° F / 175° C / Level 4.

5. Take marinated tofu and place each half in a separate mini loaf pans. Fill each with remaining marinade. Add a bay leaf to each pan.

6. Bake tofu 90 min. Remove and flip tofu pieces.

7. Bake for an additional 60–90 minutes.

COCONUT BACON BITS

MAKES 1 CUP • TIME 15 MIN

1 cup (100 g) dried coconut flakes
1/8 tsp liquid smoke
1 tsp The Wizard's Organic Worcestershire Sauce
1 tsp liquid aminos or **soy sauce**

1. Preheat oven to 350° F / 175° C / Level 4.

2. In mixing bowl, combine all ingredients. Toss until coconut flakes absorbs liquids.

3. Spread evenly on baking sheet.

4. Bake until dark brown, 8–10 min. Remove from oven, transfer to bowl and cool.

SEITAN

MAKES 2 LOAVES • TIME 2 HOURS+

1 1/2 cups (225 g) vital wheat gluten
1/4 cup (40 g) chickpea flour
1/4 cup (20 g) nutritional yeast flakes
2 tsp dried thyme
2 tsp dried rosemary
2 tsp sea salt
2 tsp onion powder
1/2 cup (120 ml) vegetable broth
2 tsp tomato puree
4 cloves garlic crushed or chopped
2 tsp olive oil

1. Mix dry ingredients together in large bowl.
2. Whisk wet ingredients with garlic in another bowl. Add to dry ingredients.
3. Mix together well and form ball of dough. If too dry, add broth 1 Tbs at a time.
4. Knead dough thoroughly for 5–10 min.
5. Cut dough in half and roll into two 3 in / 8 cm diameter loaves.

MARINADE:

4 cups (960 ml) vegetable broth
3–4 bay leaves
2 tsp dried thyme
2 tsp dried rosemary
3–4 cloves garlic chopped or crushed

1. Bring marinade ingredients to boil in saucepan. Simmer 5 min, stirring regularly.
2. Preheat oven to 350° F / 175° C / Level 4.
3. Wrap seitan loaves in damp cheesecloth and place in glassware dish.
4. Pour marinade into dish to cover seitan.
5. Bake 2 hours, turning after 1 hour.

CHEESY SAUCE

MAKES ABOUT 3 CUPS • TIME 15 MIN

1/4 cup (60 ml) olive oil
1/4 cup (40 g) flour
2 1/2 cups (600 ml) almond milk
1 1/2 tsp sea salt
1/2 tsp pepper
1 Tbs garlic powder
2 tsp onion powder
1 tsp brown mustard
1 cup (80 g) nutritional yeast flakes

1. Whisk oil and flour together in saucepan on medium heat, 5 min.

2. Mix in almond milk and remaining ingredients.

3. Increase heat to high. Bring to boil, stirring constantly.

4. Remove from heat, cover. Allow to set and thicken, about 5 min.

PUMPKIN PUREE

MAKES 2 CUPS • TIME 60 MIN+

1 pie pumpkin
1/8 tsp sea salt
coconut oil (refined)
1 Tbs molasses (for sweet puree)
1 Tbs maple syrup (for sweet puree)
2 Tbs veggie broth (for savory puree)

1. Preheat oven to 450° F / 230° C / Level 8.

2. Break stem off pumpkin. Cut in 8 pieces.

3. Scoop out seeds and pulp and place pumpkin pieces on cookie sheet lined with parchment paper.

4. Brush pieces with melted coconut oil and sprinkle with sea salt.

5. Roast in oven 40 min.

6. Allow to cool to room temperature, 20–30 min.

7. Scoop pumpkin away from skin and place in food processor.

8. Add 1 Tbs each molasses and maple syrup for use in sweet dishes, or 2 Tbs veggie broth for savory dishes.

9. Puree in food processor or blender on high, about 1 min.

STUFFING

SERVES 4 • TIME 30 MIN

4 cups (300 g) fresh bread chopped
2 Tbs olive oil
1 Tbs dried rosemary
1/2 tsp garlic powder
1/2 tsp dried parsley
1/2 tsp sea salt
1/2 tsp black pepper
1 tsp dried thyme
1/4 tsp paprika
1 stalk celery Finely chopped
1 cup (60 ml) veggie broth (page 159)
1 Tbs vegan margarine

1. Preheat oven to 350° F / 175° C / Level 4.

2. Toss bread pieces, olive oil, rosemary, garlic powder, parsley, salt, pepper, thyme and paprika in large mixing bowl until bread is evenly coated.

3. Place on baking sheet. Bake until crispy, about 5 min. Transfer to mixing bowl.

4. Heat veggie broth on high heat in pot. Add margarine and stir until melted. Remove from heat.

5. Add chopped celery to bread pieces. Pour veggie broth over croutons and mix well. Place in 8 x 8 in (20 x 20 cm) glassware baking dish and spread evenly.

6. Bake another 20 min.

ALMOND MILK

MAKES 4 CUPS / 1 L • TIME 60 MIN+

1 cup (170 g) almonds
4 cups (960 ml) water
1–2 dates for sweetness OPTIONAL
1/8 tsp vanilla extract OPTIONAL

1. Bring water to boil in pot. Turn heat off. Add almonds. Let sit 1 hour.
   For raw almond milk, soak almonds in water for 8 hours or overnight.

2. Blend almonds and water (and dates and vanilla, if desired) in high-powered
   blender (e.g. Blendtec) until smooth, about 60 sec.

3. Line a bowl with cheesecloth. Pour almond milk into cheesecloth to strain almond
   and date pieces. Gently squeeze contents of cheesecloth to remove liquid.

SWEET SEITAN

MAKES 2 LOAVES • TIME 2 HOURS+

1 1/2 cups (225 g) vital wheat gluten
1/2 cup (75 g) chickpea flour
1/4 cup (20 g) nutritional yeast flakes
2 Tbs brown sugar
1/2 Tbs mesquite powder
1/2 Tbs garlic powder
1/2 tsp turmeric
1/8 tsp black pepper
1 Tbs The Wizard's Organic Worcestershire Sauce
1 cup (240 ml) veggie broth
1 Tbs liquid aminos or **soy sauce**
1 tsp liquid smoke
2 cloves garlic chopped or crushed

1. In mixing bowl, whisk all dry ingredients together well.

2. In separate bowl, whisk wet ingredients and garlic.

3. Mix together to form a dough ball. Knead it thoroughly, 5–10 min. Let rest 20 min.

4. Cut seitan in half and form two 3 in (8 cm) loaves.

MARINADE:

1 1/2 cups (360 ml) veggie broth (page 159)
2 onions chopped
4 cloves garlic crushed or finely chopped
2 bay leaves
1/4 cup (60 g) brown sugar
1/2 tsp chili powder
1 Tbs dried parsley
1/2 tsp dried thyme
1 Tbs soy sauce
1 Tbs molasses
2 cups (480 ml) water

1. Bring marinade ingredients to boil in saucepan. Simmer 5 min, stirring regularly.

2. Preheat oven to 350° F / 175° C / Level 4.

3. Wrap seitan loaves in damp cheesecloth and place in glassware dish.

4. Pour marinade into dish to cover seitan. Cover.

5. Bake 2 hours, turning and removing cover after 1 hour.

VEGAN MAYONNAISE

MAKES 1 CUP • TIME 10 MIN

6 oz (170 g) silken tofu
2 Tbs olive oil
2 tsp apple cider vinegar
1 tsp sea salt
1/8 tsp black pepper
1 Tbs spicy brown mustard
1/8 tsp dried dill
1/2 tsp garlic powder
1/2 tsp onion powder
2 Tbs soy milk

\. Blend all ingredients in a high-powered blender (e.g. Blendtec) or food processor until smooth and creamy, about 30–45 sec.

MAPLE GLAZED TOFU

MAKES 16 OZ / 450 G • TIME 30 MIN+

16 oz (450 g) extra firm tofu
1 cup (240 ml) water
1/4 cup (60 ml) olive oil
juice of 1 lemon
3 cloves garlic Finely chopped
1 sprig fresh rosemary Finely chopped
1/4 cup (60 ml) maple syrup
1 tsp salt
2 Tbs liquid aminos or **soy sauce**

1. Whisk all ingredients together in mixing bowl or casserole dish.

2. Add the tofu, mix and turn several times to coat. Marinate overnight.

MAPLE GLAZE:

3 Tbs maple syrup
2 tsp Dijon mustard
1 tsp hot sauce
1/8 tsp Chinese 5-spice seasoning

1. Mix all glaze ingredients together in small bowl.

2. Remove tofu from marinade and place on grill or a well-oiled skillet on high heat.

3. Cook each side about 3 min, brushing on glaze liberally.

PIZZA DOUGH

MAKES DOUGH FOR 1 LARGE PIZZA • 90 MIN

1 cup (240 ml) warm water
1 Tbs dry active yeast
2 Tbs sugar
1 tsp sea salt
2 Tbs olive oil
1 cup (150 g) bread flour
2 cups (300 g) flour

1. In mixing bowl add warm water. Stir in sugar and yeast.
   Cover with towel and let sit 5 min.

2. Add oil, salt and flour. Stir together until it forms a ball. Flour countertop and knead dough until it's not sticky. Add more flour gradually if needed.

3. Roll dough into tight ball and place in mixing bowl lightly coated in oil. Rub oil on dough ball. Cover with plastic wrap and let rise at room temperature 60 min.

4. Press dough down and roll into another ball or cut in half and make two balls. Allow to rise prior to use, or refrigerate for later use.

INDY'S DOG TREATS

MAKES 18 BISCUITS • TIME 60 MIN

1/4 cup (60 g) peanut butter
1/4 cup (60 ml) sunflower oil
12 oz (340 g) silken tofu
2 bananas
1/4 cup (35 g) flax seeds gRound
1/4 cup (20 g) nutritional yeast flakes
2 1/2 cups (375 g) whole wheat flour
1/8 tsp cinnamon

1. Preheat oven to 350° F / 175° C / Level 4.

2. In mixing bowl, add peanut butter, oil, silken tofu and bananas. Mash it all together.

3. Add flax seeds, nutritional yeast and cinnamon. Stir together well.

4. Add flour, mix well. If dough is too wet, add another 1/2 cup (75 g).

5. Sprinkle flour on counter and roll dough out flat, about 1/4 in (1/2 cm) thick.

6. Use a dog bone cookie cutter, cut out treats and add them to parchment paper lined baking sheet.

7. Bake in oven 40 min.

8. Let cool and give to your favorite pup.

INDY'S DOG FOOD

MAKES ABOUT 18 CUPS • TIME 60 MIN

1 cup (200 g) brown rice*
1 cup (100 g) oats*
1 cup (200 g) barley*
6 cups (1400 ml) water
1 large sweet potato chopped
4 medium carrots chopped
1/4 cup (60 ml) canola or **sunflower oil**
2 tsp dried rosemary
1/4 cup (40 g) sunflower seeds ground
1/4 cup (35 g) flax seeds ground
12 oz (340 g) silken tofu mashed
2 bananas mashed
1 can (15 oz / 425 g) pumpkin puree
2 cups (200 g) frozen peas
1/2 cup (40 g) nutritional yeast flakes
1/4 cup (60 g) peanut butter

1. In large pot, bring water to a boil.

2. Add brown rice, oats and barley. (*Use amount of your choice of each, as long as it totals about 3 cups.)

3. Stir in sweet potato, carrots and oil. Cover pot and reduce heat to medium low. Cook 20 min, stirring ocassionally.

4. Add rosemary, sunflower seeds, flax seeds and tofu. Stir.

5. Reduce heat to low, cover and let simmer another 20 min.

6. Mix in bananas, pumpkin puree, peas, nutritional yeast and peanut butter.

7. Stir well. Remove from heat. Cover.

8. Let it cool down, feed to pup.

9. Store the rest in sealed container in the refrigerator.

INDY'S PUMPKIN BISCUITS

MAKES 18 BISCUITS • TIME 50 MINS

15 oz (425 g) pumpkin puree (page 169)
1/4 cup (35 g) flax seeds ground
1/2 cup (50 g) oats
1/4 cup (60 ml) sunflower oil
1 Tbs molasses
2 1/4 cups (340 g) whole wheat flour

1. Preheat oven to 350° F / 175° C / Level 4.

2. In mixing bowl, add pumpkin puree, flaxseeds, oats, oil and molasses. Mash it all together.

3. Add flour, mix well. If dough is too wet, add another 1/4 cup (40 g).

4. Sprinkle flour on counter and roll dough out flat, about 1/4 in (1/2 cm) thick.

5. Using dog bone cookie cutter, cut treats and arrange on a parchment paper lined baking sheet.

6. Bake in oven for 40 min.

7. Let cool and give to your favorite pup.

THANK YOU...

Mom, **Dad**, **Pat**, **Brian**, **Kelly**, **Mary**, **Dan Carrigan**,
Matt & Bette, **Ma & Pa Tedd**, **Rob & Ali Kramer**,
Justin P. Moore (The Lotus and the Artichoke),
Strong Hearts Café, **Sarah Liddle** (Sugar Mamas),
Cody Snyder, **Colleen Holland** (VegNews), **Nick Canino**,
Sussanna, **Tina & Kandice Gravatt**, **Valerie Garman**,
Jens Neumann, **Joachim Hiller**, **Bobcat Goldthwait**,
Jasmin (Baking the Law) and **Terry H. Romero**.

Special thanks to all of our Kickstarter backers,
YouTube subscribers and Facebook followers!

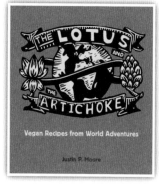

Uschi Herzer & Joachim Hiller
**Das Ox-Kochbuch 5
Kochen ohne Knochen**
Mehr als 200 vegane
Punk-Rezepte

192 Seiten • €9,90 (D)
ISBN 978-3-931555-28-3

Patrick Bolk (Hg.)
**Ab heute vegan –
So klappt dein Umstieg**
Ein Wegweiser durch
den veganen Alltag

144 Seiten • ca. €12,90 (D)
ISBN 978-3-95575-010-7

Justin P. Moore
The Lotus and the Artichoke
Vegan Recipes from
World Adventures
(English Edition)

216 Pages • €19,90 (D)
ISBN 978-3-95575-012-1